A Clear View

The Formation and Impact of Worldview

Keith Ogorek
Zionsville Fellowship

Bloomington, IN Milton Keynes, UK

AuthorHouse™
1663 Liberty Drive, Suite 200
Bloomington, IN 47403
www.authorhouse.com
Phone: 1-800-839-8640

AuthorHouse™ UK Ltd.
500 Avebury Boulevard
Central Milton Keynes, MK9 2BE
www.authorhouse.co.uk
Phone: 08001974150

First published by AuthorHouse 10/9/2006

ISBN: 1-4259-5371-9 (sc)

Printed in the United States of America
Bloomington, Indiana

This book is printed on acid-free paper.

DEDICATION

To my wife, Becky, who has supported and encouraged me to pursue my calling

To Tom Streeter for his passion to develop men of the church who live with the Upper and Lower story in balance

To Eric Bobbitt who was faithful and passionate about developing the curriculum that make up the lessons in the Learners for Life binder

To all the men of Zionsville Fellowship who have faithfully and enthusiastically risen early to meet together and "sharpen iron."

A Special Thank You to: Deb Bissell for her tireless effort in preparing the manuscript; Laura Dunshee, Dave Herbon, and Jay Parks for proofing the manuscript and providing insightful comments that improved the work; Ayrika Gunn for editing the original manuscript and creating the artwork for the book; Scott Eckart whose thinking and insights helped shape the approach to the Truth and Knowing chapters.

PREFACE

I heard recently that about 175,000 books are published each year. So why was this book necessary? Good question.

To begin with, I did not set out to write a book. I was meeting with a group of men from 6:00 to 8:00 a.m. who were part of the Men's Discipleship ministry at our church. This group, like others in our church, makes a commitment to meet together 64 times over a two-year period to study church history, theology, and worldview. In addition, each man works to develop his testimony, and better understand his calling, spiritual gifts, and Style of Influence.

It was in these groups that these chapters were born. As a staff, we were searching for a more effective way to teach worldview. We found many excellent books that identify types of worldviews, such as humanism or pragmatism. However, we could not find a text that talked about how a person's worldview was formed. Believe me, we looked.

There are a number of books that do an excellent job of outlining the progression of philosophical thought over time. However, for men who had no background in philosophy, the material was often confusing or overwhelming.

So I decided to write reading material for the lessons we were doing each week, but then as the chapters for this book. Those who know philosophy far better than I may think the content is too simple. Those who have studied worldview previously may also think I have not covered certain topics in enough detail. But remember, the book is not written for the philosopher or worldview scholar. Rather it is intended for those who have not been exposed to these ideas before. It provides an introduction to the idea of worldview and gives a framework from which to understand the related concepts.

I trust as you digest this material you will find the information helpful and encouraging and that, most importantly, it will compel you to read more.

A Clear View

1

—⊷⟡⟵—

INTRODUCTION TO WORLDVIEW

Everyone, whether he be a plowman or banker, clerk or captain, citizen or ruler, is, in a real sense a philosopher. Being human, having a highly sensitive brain and nervous system, he must think; and thinking is the pathway to philosophy.

The world in which we live will not let us rest. It keeps prodding us, challenging us with problems to be solved, demanding that we act wisely or be destroyed by the forces which inhabit our world. In this way experiences are born—hungers and satisfactions, pains and pleasures, sights, feelings, sounds and a host of others.

But we cannot be content with a mass of unrelated experiences scattered at random throughout life. We must take experiences and weave them into some kind of pattern....

Your philosophy then is the meaning which the world has for you. It is the answer to the question, "Why?" Having fitted your experiences into a whole, having related them to each other, you say of the world, "This is the way things fit together. This is the world as I understand it."

S. E. Frost
Basic Teachings of the Great Philosophers[1]

Think about the last time you put on a pair of glasses. No matter if they were reading, prescription or sun glasses, they affected how you saw and interacted with the world and people around you. Furthermore, the characteristics of the lenses affected your view. The tint, thickness and contour all worked together to create a grid through which you saw the world. Change any one characteristic of the lens and

1

it changes your view. For example, take a clear lens and add a blue tint and you see the world differently. Increase the thickness of the lens and your view changes again. That's similar to how a person's worldview works. **A worldview is like a set of glasses through which you see and interact with the world and people around you**. **Although everyone does not wear real glasses,** *every person has a worldview.*

This idea is not new. The German philosopher Immanuel Kant first used the term, *Weltanshauung* (Velt-awn-sha-uung), which is German for worldview, in his book *The Critique of Judgment* published in 1790. It was not a significant term at the time. In fact, it was only used once in his writing and meant, "an intuition of the world that we receive through sense perception." It did not have a philosophical definition at the time. However, it was quickly picked up by other philosophers who came after him, including Friedrich Schelling who defined the term as "the self-realized productive and conscious way of apprehending and interpreting the universe of beings." From there, almost every important German thinker began to use the term in his writing, and the concept of worldview was further developed and spread throughout Europe.[2]

Christian philosophers, such as James Orr, first used the term around 1900. However, it wasn't until the 1960s that the wider evangelical world began to take this idea of worldview more seriously.[3] Francis Schaeffer in his books, *The God Who Was There* and *How Should We Then Live?*, challenged evangelicals to think about the importance and implications of worldview. His insights regarding how philosophical ideas developed over time and profoundly influenced the culture served as a siren call to the Christian world to wake up and engage, not withdraw, from culture. (It's worth noting that Schaeffer's work was not warmly embraced by all Christian leaders at the time.)

Since then, important contributions to the study of worldview from a Christian vantage point have been made by a number of authors. Among them are *Understanding the Times* by David Noebel, *Lifeviews* by R.C. Sproul, *The Universe Next Door* by James Sire, *How Now Shall We Live* by Chuck Colson and Nancy Pearcey, and *Mars Hill Audio Journal*, an audio magazine by Ken Myers. Each of these works helps us:

1. Gain a more thorough understanding of the concept of worldview and its impact
2. Develop a more precise understanding of a Christian worldview
3. Identify differences among competing worldviews

Those are objectives of this work as well. Learning about these ideas will help us better engage in the dialogue of the culture and more effectively communicate the truth of the gospel into every area of life. Our goal is not just to know more, but rather to learn for the purpose of becoming a person of influence in our families, churches, schools, work places, and communities.

The apostle Paul gives us an excellent example of why that is important in Acts 17. Here we read about Paul's engagement with the people at Mars Hill.

> [16] *While Paul was waiting for them in Athens, he was deeply distressed to see that the city was full of idols.* [17] *So he argued in the synagogue with the Jews and the devout persons, and also in the marketplace every day with those who happened to be there.* [18] *Also some Epicurean and Stoic philosophers debated with him. Some said, "What does this babbler want to say?" Others said, "He seems to be a proclaimer of foreign divinities." (This was because he was telling the good news about Jesus and the resurrection.)* [19] *So they took him and brought him to the Areopagus and asked him, "May we know what this new teaching is that you are presenting?* [20] *It sounds rather strange to us, so we would like to know what it means."* [21] *Now all*

the Athenians and the foreigners living there would spend their time in nothing but telling or hearing something new.

[22] Then Paul stood in front of the Areopagus and said, "Athenians, I see how extremely religious you are in every way. [23] For as I went through the city and looked carefully at the objects of your worship, I found among them an altar with the inscription, 'To an unknown god.' What therefore you worship as unknown, this I proclaim to you. [24] The God who made the world and everything in it, he who is Lord of heaven and earth, does not live in shrines made by human hands, [25] nor is he served by human hands, as though he needed anything, since he himself gives to all mortals life and breath and all things. [26] From one ancestor he made all nations to inhabit the whole earth, and he allotted the times of their existence and the boundaries of the places where they would live, [27] so that they would search for God and perhaps grope for him and find him—though indeed he is not far from each one of us. [28] For 'In him we live and move and have our being'; as even some of your own poets have said, For we too are his offspring.'

[29] Since we are God's offspring, we ought not to think that the deity is like gold, or silver, or stone, an image formed by the art and imagination of mortals. [30] While God has overlooked the times of human ignorance, now he commands all people everywhere to repent, [31] because he has fixed a day on which he will have the world judged in righteousness by a man whom he has appointed, and of this he has given assurance to all by raising him from the dead."

[32] When they heard of the resurrection of the dead, some scoffed; but others said, "We will hear you again about this." [33] At that point Paul left them. [34] But some of them joined him and became believers, including Dionysius the Areopagite and a woman named Damaris, and others with them.[4]

At the beginning of this text, we see Paul at work in the synagogues among the religious people in Athens. However in the latter part of the account, we find Paul in dialogue with the Epicureans and Stoics. These two groups of people represented two dominant worldviews in that day. But look at what Paul does. Though his goal was to preach the gospel, he does not start there. Instead, **he begins his conversation from *their* understanding of the world, not his.** He acknowledges their idols to "the unknown God." Then he walks them from their understanding of God and the world to the gospel and the person of Jesus Christ. What a masterful discussion! What an example! Paul wasn't simply satisfied to understand their worldviews and how they were different from his. It's clear he used his understanding of philosophy and worldview to engage the people of his day for the purpose of communicating the truth of the risen Christ, which should be our goal as well.

If we simply study worldview to increase our knowledge, but fail to use that knowledge to communicate the reality of the Christian life at every point of culture we touch, there is the potential for us to live in an "intellectual gated community."

In the movie *Sister Act*, there's a wonderful example of what that can look like and why it's not desirable. The actress, Whoopi Goldberg, plays a Vegas lounge singer who witnesses a murder and is placed in a witness protection program to keep her safe until she can testify at the trial. The police hide her, disguised as a nun, in an inner-city convent. The convent is safe and secure because the gates are always padlocked, and there is very little contact with outside world. Within the walls, the nuns have their own community and conduct their religious duty, while the community around them is broken down and decaying. Truth and beauty exist but are sealed off in the safety of the gated community. Whoopi helps the others realize their purpose is to impact the people around them by taking what they know about truth and beauty into the world. So they throw open the gates and begin engaging with the people of the neighborhood. The nuns begin serving and the community is transformed.

I think this movie can help us see that, if we are not intentional in our worldview study, we could end up like the nuns inside the gates. We may understand a Christian worldview, be able to point out the flaws in other views, and perform our religious duty within our own community but fail to take that knowledge into the streets to transform the community. We'll live sealed-off lives, isolated in our own subculture, while the culture around us decays. We'll know more, but we'll simply use our knowledge to label people and move on, instead of loving them and communicating the truth and beauty of the gospel at every point of culture we touch.

So Where Do We Start?

Once you accept the idea that everyone has a worldview, it is extremely helpful to understand how a person's worldview is formed. Even though there are predominant worldviews which we can identify, a worldview is actually very personal and dynamic. By understanding this personal and dynamic nature, we can avoid stereotyping people and relate to them as unique individuals.

What then are the elements that make up a person's worldview? In *The Universe Next Door*, James Sire defines worldview as "...a set of presuppositions (or assumptions) which we hold consciously or subconsciously about the basic makeup of our world."[5] What are these presuppositions that make a person's worldview? I would like to suggest there are three major components that contribute to the formation of a worldview.

The first component is a person's thoughts about **God**. Does He *exist*? What are His *attributes*? Is He *knowable*? Every person you know has some opinion or answer to these questions about God. However, most people have not thought very long or hard about their answers. In many cases, their answers are closer to what they want God to be than what He really is.

The second component is a person's thoughts about **Man**. Is man basically *good or evil*? Is he *fated* or does he have *free will*? Is man *immortal* and, if so, what happens when he dies? Where does *authority* over man lie? These are questions every person has answered in some way in his or her own mind, though it is unlikely they have thought very significantly about their conclusions.

The final component that contributes to the formulation of worldview is a person's thoughts about **Existence**. How did it all *begin* and how will it *end*? What is the nature and relationship of *good* and *evil*? What is the nature and relationship between the *material* and *immaterial* worlds? How do we *know* anything and can we know *truth*? Just like with the questions relating to God and Man, everybody holds some opinion or answer to these questions as well.

At the point where these three components – God, Man and Existence – converge, a person's worldview takes shape. Figure 1 below illustrates how these components relate to one another to help form a person's worldview.

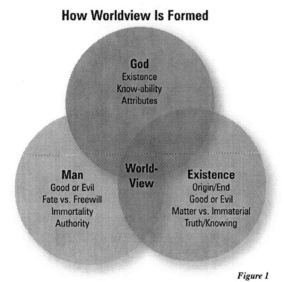

How Worldview Is Formed

God
Existence
Know-ability
Attributes

Man
Good or Evil
Fate vs. Freewill
Immortality
Authority

World-View

Existence
Origin/End
Good or Evil
Matter vs. Immaterial
Truth/Knowing

Figure 1

Change any one element and it influences the other components dramatically. For example, if a person is a deist (Figure 3), he believes in the existence of God, but the impact of that conviction on his thinking about man and existence would be very different than in Figure 1. If a person is an atheist (Figure 2), he assumes God doesn't exist so his conclusions about the issues related to man and existence would be very different from a person who believes in the reality of God.

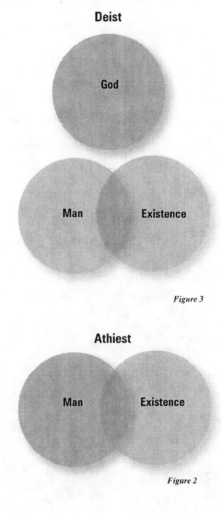

Figure 3

Figure 2

Science can tell you what and how, but it cannot tell you why.

But then say, by the grace of God, the atheist becomes a Christian. His worldview would change and be represented by Figure 1. His inclusion of God into his worldview would influence his thoughts about the immortality of man, the beginning and end of existence, as well as every other thought he has about man and existence.

However, when we talk with people, we rarely, if ever, talk about worldview. Instead, we converse about topics such as work, money, family, marriage, sex, sports, etc. So what is the connection between a person's worldview and those topics? Figure 4 helps illustrate this relationship between the two. Along with a worldview, every person has a "**Life Picture.**"

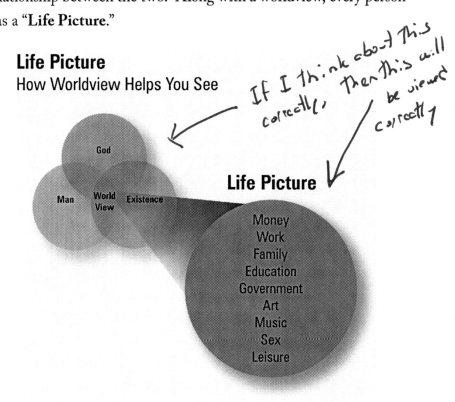

Life Picture
How Worldview Helps You See

If I think about this correctly, Then this will be viewed correctly

God

Man   World View   Existence

Life Picture

Money
Work
Family
Education
Government
Art
Music
Sex
Leisure

Figure 4

A Life Picture is the perspective or conviction we have about the common things of life that is informed and influenced by our worldview. This is an important concept because our contact with people is usually with respect to the way they see their Life Picture, not their worldview. In other words, people more commonly express how they see money, work, government, sex, etc., rather than their worldview. However, if we understand how worldview influences their day-to-day life issues, we can often discern their worldview just by listening to how they talk about the elements in their Life Picture. This is extremely helpful if we want to do as Paul did on Mars Hill and begin a conversation from the other person's understanding of the world, not ours.

Let's Start with the Questions

As we begin our study of worldview, we will start by examining the key questions in each component of a person's worldview. How do we know anything and what is truth? What is the relationship between the material and immaterial worlds? How did the universe begin and how will it end? Is man fated or does he have free will? What is the ultimate authority in man's life? What happens when man dies? What is the nature and relationship between good and evil?

These are key questions philosophers and theologians have been wrestling with for thousands of years. We will look at some of the answers major thinkers have offered to these subjects. More importantly, we will wrestle with these questions ourselves as we strive to articulate our own personal philosophy which informs our worldview and shapes the elements in our Life Picture.

It cannot be too often repeated that philosophy is everybody's business. To be a human being is to be endowed with the proclivity to philosophize. To some degree we all engage in philosophical thought in the course of our daily lives.

Acknowledging it is not enough. It is also necessary to understand why this is so and what philosophy's business is.

The answer in a word is ideas. In two words, it is great ideas— the ideas basic and indispensable to understanding ourselves, our society and the world in which we live.

These ideas, as we shall see presently, constitute the vocabulary of everyone's thought. Everyone uses them in ordinary conversation. But everyone does not understand them as well as they can be understood, nor has everyone pondered sufficiently the questions raised....

To do that and to think one's way through to some resolution of the conflicting answers to these questions is to philosophize.

Mortimer Adler
Six Great Ideas[6]

DISCUSSION QUESTIONS

1) What does it mean that a worldview is personal and dynamic?

2) What influences do you think contribute to how a person's worldview is formed?

3) Which question in the worldview circles, in your opinion, has the most influence in shaping a person's worldview? Why?

4) Which of the issues in the Life Picture diagram do you think is most important? Why?

For personal reflection: Take some time to reflect on how you answered those questions. Would the non-Christians you come in contact with know you are a Christian? If so, why? If not, why?

2

———— ◆ ————

TRUTH AND KNOWING—PART I

Whence come our ideas? Are they born with us and do they become conscious in time or do we get them from sense experiences? Or does some god reveal them to us?

S. E. Frost
Basic Teachings of the Great Philosopher[7]

Since philosophers first began searching for answers about life, they have wrestled with two key questions that lay the foundation for developing conclusions about most everything else.

The first question is, **"How do we know?"** The second is, **"What can we know?"** These two questions form the basis for the field of study in philosophy known as **epistemology**. This discipline is defined as the branch of philosophy that studies the nature of knowledge, its presuppositions and foundations, and its extent and validity.[8] Now let's take a moment to consider the two key questions.

How Do We Know?

From the early Greeks to modern man, philosophers have continually pondered the question, **"How do we know what we know?"** Ancient Greek philosophers offered two competing answers. Stoics and Epicureans (see Acts 17) held the position that all knowledge was received by the senses. The soul, for them, is an empty slate at birth and receives impressions, which are then organized into ideas. Since they believe these ideas come through experiences, they were often referred to as "empiricists."[9]

In the other camp, were the "rationalists." They taught that ideas are resident in man at birth and experience simply awakens them. Plato was one of the leading advocates of this position and, as you can imagine, there were some lively debates between those who held such opposing views. In fact, S. E. Frost suggests, "The progress of philosophy is more or less a battle between various forms of these two major positions...."[10]

So which position is correct? I believe each makes an important contribution to answering the question, "How do we know?" On their own, neither one provides a complete answer. That's because a Christian worldview suggests that we can know things by three means: **cognitively, empirically** and **by revelation**. Let's examine each of these in more detail.

Cognitive refers to things we know intuitively or without learning. They exist in our minds and come from within. For example, a baby does not need to learn hunger or to cry. That's "hardwired" in. Other things we know are **empirical**. This refers to what we've learned through sensory experience or observation. An infant doesn't need training to know hunger, but he does need to learn how to use a fork or chop sticks to feed himself. Empirical knowledge usually comes from trial and error and experimentation and repetition. The third way we know is by **revelation.** For example, if we are going to know anything about God, it requires revelation or a revealing of truths about Himself. Then as we know Him, we can order our lives according to His will. Without revelation, it is impossible for us to know anything about God. Figure 5 illustrates how all three work together to help us understand what we know.

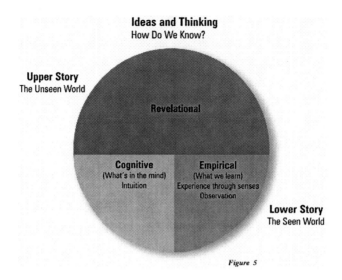

Figure 5

We will examine this in more detail in the next chapter, but it is important to note that one of the results of post-Enlightenment thinking has been a rejection of the premise that we can know anything above the horizontal line or what's called the "upper story." This is a key difference between a Christian worldview and the humanist views that are predominate in our culture today. In many ways, this difference is the fork in the road where divergent worldviews begin.

What Can We Know?

Once we arrive at a conclusion about how we know, it's also important to consider the question, **"What can we know?"** In fact, historically this has been one of the primary issues thinkers have addressed. In the sixth and fifth centuries BC, two Greek philosophers, Herodotus and Parmenides, offered two very different points of view.

Herodotus noted that the world we encountered is in constant flux or change. The seasons change, people grow older, new plants emerge from the winter snow. He was said to have claimed that you can't step in the same river twice. That observation captured Herodotus' view that the world does not stay put. Because the world doesn't stay constant, it is impossible to achieve true knowledge of it. The things we thought we knew are no longer the same when we examine them again. The constant flux keeps us from understanding the true nature of the world.[11]

If you understand Herodotus's view, you can see how it affects his conviction about truth. His claim was that we could not know "the true nature of the universe." Therefore, truth is not objective and fixed, but rather changing. Considered on its own, that view may not seem that significant. However, it has profound implications when it works its way down to matters such as the nature of God or moral law. Not everyone agreed with Herodotus in his day.

Parmenides offered a radically different conception of our world. He argued that the world really is a single unchanging, infinitely large entity. But this world cannot be known by the senses because our senses tell us that there are numerous things–things that constantly change. Parmenides concludes that knowledge is arrived at not through the senses but through reason.[12]

Contrary to Herodotus, Parmenides suggested that the world was unchanging or fixed, and reason, not our senses, was needed to understand the world around us. So which is it? Changing or fixed? Senses or reason? The debate continued. Socrates, who lived from 470 to 399 BC, was the next major Greek thinker to offer an answer. He used an approach, which was named after him, called the Socratic Method.

This involves persistent, relentless questioning, designed to force people into examining their own beliefs. This intellectual dissection forced people to recognize that they didn't know as much as they thought they did and exposed contradictory beliefs. Socrates himself was proclaimed by the oracle at Delphi to be the wisest of humans, but humbly claimed that the only thing he knew was that he knew nothing; whereas other people were equally ignorant but thought themselves wise.[13]

One of Socrates's students was Plato, who recorded Socrates's conversations and reported them in a series of dialogues. In addition, Plato developed one of the most important postulations about the nature of the universe and what we can know.

Plato's most important legacy is his theory of forms. To set the stage for this theory, recall the views of Herodotus and Parmenides. Herodotus argued that if the world is constantly in flux, there can be no knowledge of the world. Parmenides described reality as an unchanging limitless entity. Plato synthesized these views.

What Plato describes is a world with two layers. One layer is the world revealed to us by our senses. The other, a world with ordinary physical objects which are constantly changing. Plato says there are no truths to be found in this world, only appearance or illusion. The other layer is the realm of what is real; what really exists. This is Plato's world of forms or universals.[14]

But Plato wasn't the only one to advance a widely accepted theory about the nature of the world and our ability to know it. One of his students was Aristotle, who lived from 384 to 322 BC and he also became a philosopher of significant influence. Both Plato and Aristotle agreed that there were forms or universals that have an objective existence and do not change. However, where Plato insisted these forms (universals) are not fully present in material things (particulars), Aristotle said they were. Where Plato insisted we cannot know the universals fully by studying particulars,

Aristotle suggested that study of particulars will in fact lead us to an understanding of the universals. In other words, the objective world of forms and universals is not something illusive or something separate from matter, but *something we can know.*

For approximately 700 years, from 500 to 1200 AD, Plato's ideas and thinking dominated both western culture and the Church. Then education was re-born around 1000 AD through the work of men historians have dubbed, the Scholastics. This group, which included men such as Peter Abelard, Peter Lombard, Bernard of Clairvaux, John of Salisbury, St. Bonaventure, Albertus Magnus, Duns Scotus, William of Ockham and most notably, Thomas Aquinas (1225-1274), helped rekindle a love for learning and caused a shift from Plato's ideas to Aristotle's. In fact, to be able to understand how modern man answers the questions "How do we know?", and "What can we know?," it is extremely helpful to understand this shift from the "Platonic Period" (500-1200 AD) to the "Aristotelian Revolution" (1200-1500 AD) and specifically, the role Thomas Aquinas played.[15]

Among his many contributions to philosophy and theology, Aquinas opened the way for a discussion about the difference and relationship between "Nature" and "Grace." This discussion centers around the perpetual and critical problem humans have had in coming to grips with our understanding of the seen and unseen world and what can we know of them.

Building from Plato and Aristotle, Aquinas described the world as having an upper story and a lower story. The upper story, which is the unseen, immaterial world of God, heaven, and grace, is understood by faith and requires revelation. The lower story, which is the material, seen world of man, earth, and nature is understood by reason and requires sensory interaction. Separating these two stories is "a line of despair." Figure 6 illustrates this relationship.[16]

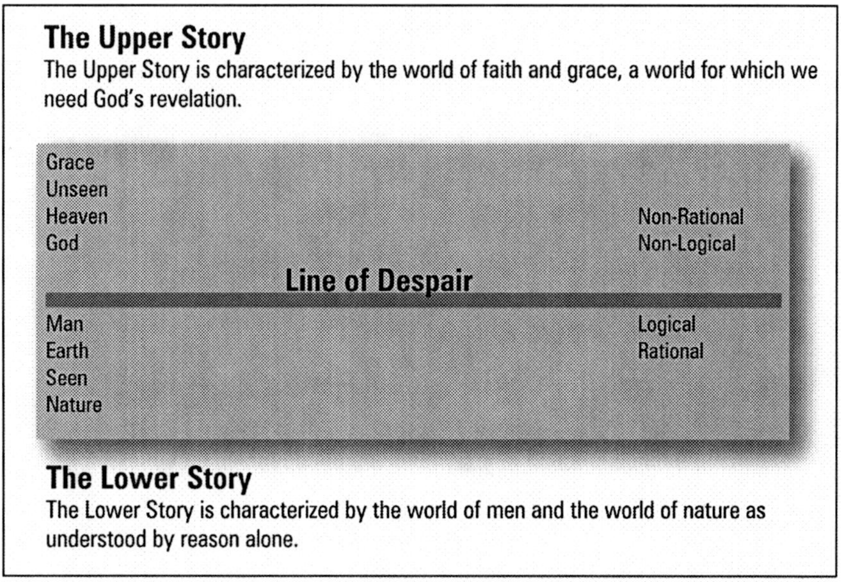

The Upper Story
The Upper Story is characterized by the world of faith and grace, a world for which we need God's revelation.

Grace	
Unseen	
Heaven	Non-Rational
God	Non-Logical

Line of Despair

Man	Logical
Earth	Rational
Seen	
Nature	

The Lower Story
The Lower Story is characterized by the world of men and the world of nature as understood by reason alone.

Figure 6

This line has been described as a "line of despair" because it has, indeed, caused great despair for people throughout history as they have struggled to answer the questions, "What can we know?" and "What is real?" Generally, man has answered those questions one of three ways:

1. Emphasize the importance of the upper story while diminishing or denying the significance of the lower story.
2. Diminish or deny the upper story while embracing the lower story.
3. Accept and embrace the existence and importance of both stories enabling a "unified field of knowledge."[17]

At its root, each person's worldview begins and follows a particular trajectory based on one of these three options. Figure 7 shows different worldviews that derive from an emphasis on one story over the other.

Upper Story Dominant Worldviews

Mystic, Gnostic, Spiritualist
Romantic, Existentialist

Line of Despair

Rationalist, Pragmatist,
Logician, Naturalist, Atheist

Lower Story Dominant Worldviews

Figure 7

How a person resolves this upper and lower story issue also determines how meaning, morals and absolutes are derived and what he or she believes about truth. For example, during the Platonic period, importance was given to the upper story over the lower story, or another way to say it is that grace dominated nature. As a result, art and architecture reflected "heavenly" things rather than the beauty of creation. Human beings were painted flat and without shape. The work of the monastery was thought to be of greater value than that of the marketplace. Morals were pronounced from those in the Church who served as the conduit for the upper story. However, all that began to change around 1200 AD.[18]

Propelled by the rebirth of learning and Aristotle's influence, a shift between the upper and lower stories took place during a period historians have called the Renaissance. Nature was given a more proper place. The material world was no longer despised. Creation and the human form became the objects of art. Nature now began to dominate grace and the results were significant.

Creativity in the arts, architecture, music, literature and invention flourished. The talents of men such as Dante, Leonardo da Vinci, and Michelangelo were unleashed. They produced amazing works of art and architecture and made great advancements in the physical sciences. However, near the end of this period, the pendulum had swung too far.

Man now saw nature or the lower story as superior to the upper story. This led to a view of life called humanism, where man became the reference point for all things. Morals, meaning, and absolutes were now defined by man with reference to himself instead of objective truth. Man began to distrust what he could really know above the line; or perhaps, he just trusted more in what he could know below the line by his own reason. This thinking had an impact in all areas of life, including theology, philosophy, and art.[19]

In theology, Aquinas developed arguments for natural theology, which tries to prove the existence of God by reason alone. For the first time, man was saying revelation or upper story knowledge was not needed to understand God. Philosophy began to "take wings" and was now being developed apart from revelation. Prior to these changes, philosophy always had been related to scripture and the Church, but now it was free to go in any direction it chose. Art also became autonomous and artists began to express reality as they saw fit rather than in reference to the truth of scripture or the Church. For example, in the Sistine Chapel, we see biblical figures combined with mythological characters—a depiction that would have never happened when grace policed art.[20]

Though it was manifested in many different forms, the one common element among all Renaissance thinkers and artists was a belief in, and search for, a universal truth that governs all of life and meaning. Their search was in vain because they were looking in the wrong place. The shift from an upper to lower story focus caused them to look only at man as the source of this truth and diminish the contribution of the upper story.[21]

This was certainly not Aquinas's intent when he reintroduced Aristotle's thoughts into the church and culture. In fact, Aquinas emphasized the need for what philosophers call a "unified field of knowledge" where proper emphasis is given to both grace and nature. According to Aquinas, faith and reason are both employed to help us understand the value and place of the upper and lower story. Sadly, that's not what happened. As we will see, the effects of the shift that took place during this period had an immediate impact and created intellectual aftershocks that affect us even today.

But why have we taken the time to explain this Aristotelian Revolution, and how can this knowledge be useful today? First, if you really want to understand the worldview of another person, it is extremely helpful to know where he stands on the issue of nature and grace. The way a person thinks about nature and grace helps us know where he looks for answers to big questions. Second, developing a solid, biblical Christian worldview should include a "unified field of knowledge" which embraces a proper perspective on both the upper and lower story. Third, the development of thought up to our day can be traced back to this struggle between nature and grace that Aquinas posed.

In fact, in many ways, the Reformation, which followed the Renaissance, was an attempt to restore a proper relationship between nature and grace—between the upper and lower stories. Recall that from 500-1200 AD, prominence was given to the upper story. Then, around 1200 AD there was a shift in focus to the lower story. But starting around 1500 AD, men like Luther, Calvin, and Zwingli labored to bring harmony between nature and grace and give each its appropriate place. They rejected the "religious" humanism that had crept into the church. The church and Bible were not equal in authority. It was "sola scriptura," scripture alone, which had authority and gave us substantial, but not exhaustive, information about God. Human work was not needed for salvation. It was "sola Christus," Christ alone, whose work was sufficient for salvation.

The Reformers restored grace to a position of importance, but they did not let the pendulum swing far enough to diminish nature. In fact, they saw the material world, including creation and physical activities, such as work and sex, as having a significance and importance because a good God made all those things. Just as Renaissance thinking impacted culture, so too did Reformation thought. Learning and education flourished. Creativity in art and music exploded. Just laws, civil government, and economics were birthed during this period. It was an amazing time. Reason had been revitalized during the Renaissance, but it was now tempered by revelation. Nature had dominated but was now seasoned by grace, and everyone benefited. The church, culture, government, children, and tradesmen all felt the impact of this view of life. It resulted in harmony between the two stories. Writing in his journal, Luther made this observation about the period:

> *If you read all the annals of the past, you will find no century like this since the birth of Christ. Such building and planting, such good living and dressing, such enterprise in commerce, such a stir in the arts, has not been since Christ came into the world. And how numerous are the sharp and intelligent people who leave nothing hidden and unturned: even a boy of twenty years knows more nowadays than was known formerly by twenty doctors of divinity.*[22]

It was clear to Reformation thinkers that answering the questions "how do we know?" and "what can we can know?" must be informed by both grace and nature as well as revelation and reason. The material and immaterial worlds were knowable and objective truth did exist. However, it wouldn't be long before the answers to those questions changed and once again all of culture would be impacted. We will further discuss this topic in the next chapter.

DISCUSSION QUESTIONS

1) What are the three ways we can know? Give examples of each.

2) Define and contrast how each of these philosophers answered the question, "What can we know?"
   Herodotus
   Parmenides
   Plato
   Aristotle

3) What role did Thomas Aquinas play in helping define our understanding of what we can know?

4) Describe some of the advances and creativity unleashed because of the "Aristotelian Revolution."

5) Given the Line of Despair, how did "nature" begin to consume "grace" during the Renaissance?

6) What was the result of theology, philosophy, and art becoming "autonomous" in scope?

7) What was the Reformation? What was it in response to?

8) How did the Reformers, (Luther, Calvin, et al) deal with the issue of "nature vs. grace"?

9) What evidences of the re-birth of culture came out of the Reformation?

3

TRUTH AND KNOWING—PART II

For 500 years, faith has been in retreat, abandoning the battlefield of the physical world yard by yard, until now it sits within its last defense, its final redoubt in the place of revelation, under the cloud of unknowing. Meanwhile, science, in ascendance, has swarmed across the landscape, capturing everything from quark to quasar. Yet now, even as victory seems at hand, the armies of empiricism appear confused by causality, crippled by uncertainty. Suddenly, the banner under which it fought looks indistinguishable from the torn one waving weakly above the enemies' trenches. The simple truths over which the war began now seem neither simple nor true.

What Is True
Forbes ASAP[23]

The tug-of-war between revelation and reason, nature and grace, and the upper and lower stories, which began during the Renaissance, became even more pronounced in the years that followed. As we read in the previous chapter, the Reformation was an effort to bring ways of knowing and the upper and lower stories into harmony. But by the 1700s, the pull toward reason once again captured the minds and hearts of men. During this period, which historians refer to as the Enlightenment, "leading intellectuals claimed that all life could be understood with reference to itself rather than with reference to God and the teaching of the Church."[24] According to Francis Schaeffer, "The humanistic elements which had risen during the Renaissance came to flood tide in the Enlightenment. Here was man starting from himself absolutely."[25]

As a result, reason became man's most trusted ally when it came to answering the question, *"What can we know?"* Revelation was no longer considered valid and so man's thinking shifted in three significant ways. First, one of the ways man could understand and define his existence was thrown out. The upper story was closed and man was now left to answer every question he faced from a cognitive or empirical lower story point of view. Second, when reason was elevated and revelation eliminated, it opened the door for a deistic view of life. This view accepts that God exists and created the world. However, He set it in motion and now has backed away to let it run. He has not revealed truth to men. In fact, if He is there, He has not and does not speak. Figure 8 illustrates how a deistic view contrasts with a Christian worldview.

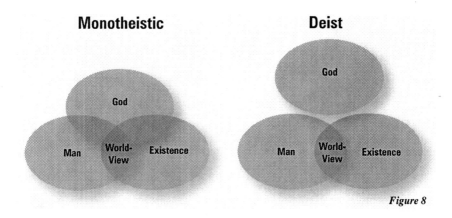

Figure 8

Notice how the top circle is there, but has no intersection with the lower two circles. In this picture, you see how life can be compartmentalized into sacred parts and secular parts; how people can live dualistically–having a "church" life and a "real" life.

The third and perhaps most important consequence of the shift in thinking about reason and revelation was it created the path for men like Immanuel Kant and George Wilhelm Frederich Hegel to introduce a philosophy and basis for modern thought that still impacts us today.

Who Is Immanuel Kant and Why Is He Important?

Although the Enlightenment lasted for only a few decades, it was perhaps one of the most important periods in the modern era because it was near the end of this time that the relationship between truth and reason started to come apart. The Enlightenment fueled a distrust of the Church and faith contributed to the view that truth could not be known by reason. During this period a fissure developed between reason and faith, but it was Immanuel Kant who drove a wedge between the two.

Kant, who lived from 1724 to 1804 constructed a theory of knowledge that excluded the possibility of knowing God (or anything above the line—which to him was God) with the mind. He introduced a "flight from knowledge," which states that the seat of faith is a person's intuition (emotions and will) and not reason. In Kant's view, reason could be applied to the natural world (lower story), but not in the supernatural world (upper story). To Kant, "faith is a matter of individual experience, a personal intuition, not an acceptance of theological propositions."[26] In his book, *Religion within the Limits of Reason Alone*, Kant argues that, "True religion is to consist of not knowing or considering what God has done for our salvation but what we must do to be worthy of it...and of whose necessity every man can become wholly certain without any Scriptural learning whatsoever.... Man himself must make or have had made himself into whatever, in a moral sense, whether good or evil, he is or is to become."[27] In these few statements we see the fruit of seeds planted during the Renaissance. Now even in religious matters, man becomes the measure. In addition, the way he finds answers to moral or religious questions changes. Objective truths that exist apart from individual preference or experience are no longer needed. Man now is free to define morality starting from himself. Prior to Kant, man depended upon reason to explore both the upper and lower stories. Now reason is put aside with reference to the upper story.

Yet as influential as Kant was, it is arguably the German philosopher George Hegel who has had the greatest impact on shaping how modern man thinks about truth and what we can know. Hegel, who lived from 1770 to 1831, introduced a way of arriving at truth called Hegel's dialectical, which "changed the world" according to Francis Schaeffer.[28] Prior to Hegel, the accepted rational understanding of the world and truth was based on the thesis/antithesis principle. This states that there are certain things which are true (absolutes) and there are certain things, which are opposite, that are not true. There are certain things which are right and others which are wrong. In classical logic, it's expressed this way: A is A, but A is not non-A.

Hegel rejected this premise. According to Hegel, a thesis is a starting point, not an end. For with every thesis comes its antithesis or opposite. If we assume the thesis to be true, then we will also encounter its opposite, or in other words, its contradiction. If we relate or unite the thesis and antithesis, we actually discover a new truth that transcends the meanings of each truth before they were united. In short, "new" truth is created through this process.

James Sire, in his book, *The Universe Next Door*, summarizes Hegel's view this way. To Hegel, ". . . the universe is steadily unfolding and so is man's understanding of it. No single proposition about reality can truly reflect what is the case. Rather in the heart of the truth one finds its opposite. This, where recognized, unfolds and stands in opposition to thesis. Yet there is truth in both thesis and antithesis and when this is perceived, a synthesis is formed and a new proposition states the truth of the newly recognized situation…thus, the universe and man's understanding of it unfolds dialectically. In short, the universe with its consciousness—man—evolves."[29]

So whereas before there was the thesis A, and its antithesis, non-A, which were both thought to be fixed and objective; now, according to Hegel, we have the thesis A, and its antithesis, non-A. When set in conflict with one another, a synthesis or new truth B comes to light. Truth, once thought to be fixed, is now accepted as evolving.

At first, this theory may seem harmless or simply philosophical banter. However, its application has had, and continues to have, profound ramifications. Karl Marx used Hegel's dialectical to create Marxism. His premise asserted that A was a lower class in society. Non-A was an upper class and the synthesis of the two was a classless society. Hegel's dialectical has also been applied to sexuality and gender. A is male. Non-A is female and the synthesis of the two is asexual or genderless. The rock star Marilyn Manson would be an example of someone who expresses this synthesis.

The point is not for us to become an expert in Hegel's dialectical but rather to understand the consequences of this view of truth. First, truth is not fixed but is always evolving and being discovered. So the goal is always to discover a "new" truth which is assumed to be better than the "old." Second, Biblical Christianity is based on the thesis/antithesis principle. Often the conflict between a Christian worldview and other worldviews begins at the point of how we arrive at truth. (One could argue the battle between evolution and creationism is, at its root, a battle about how truth is understood, not just about science.) Third, Hegel's idea leads to a view that truth is not objective and does not exist apart from experience. It is relative and discovered or realized as a result of experience and through reason. This again sets up a conflict with a Christian worldview, which holds that there are objective truths that exist apart from experience and do not originate from man.

The Importance of Hegel

Why is understanding Hegel important? It's important because modern man is more influenced by Hegel's view of truth than history's, primarily because Hegel's thinking dominated philosophy departments and university campuses in Europe and the U.S. through the mid 1900s.[30] His thinking shaped a generation's view of what we could know and how we know. So as we relate to people today, we probably won't encounter the name Hegel, but we will continually bump into his synthesized view of truth. In fact, Schaeffer has said, "One cannot understand modern man in philosophy, in the other disciplines, in morals, in political thought, without understanding that Hegel has won."[31]

Kierkegaard and the Birth of Existentialism

As influential as Hegel was, not everyone accepted his view of truth and reason. The Danish philosopher and theologian Sören Kierkegaard (1813-55) did not reject Hegel's view completely but suggested that you cannot arrive at synthesis (truth) through reason. Instead, you achieve anything of real importance by a **leap of faith.** In other words, Kierkegaard held that if rational man wants to deal with the really important issues of human life (such as purpose, significance, love), he must discard rational thought and make a non-rational "leap of faith."

This idea had significant implications. First, it further clouded man's view of truth because Kierkegaard held the position that the only thing we can "know" is experience. Second, his philosophical system made religion a very personal matter because the "leap" was made by the individual, not the Church. This too affected how truth was understood. As S. E. Frost points out, "If religion then is a purely personal matter, truth is clearly subjective, quite separate from the 'truth' of religious doctrine, for the truth of man's experience must emerge from his faithfulness to his own unique identity."[32] Faith had been divorced from reason some time ago, but after Kierkegaard, truth was now wed to personal experience. This produced a third ramification. A foundation was laid for modern existentialism. In fact, many historians consider Kierkegaard the father of this view of the world.

What Is Existentialism?

Existentialism is a philosophy or worldview that purports "meaning can only be applied to what already *is* within an individual's experience."[33] Therefore, meaning is found in the experience or the moment you live, rather than in objective truths.

Interestingly, both atheistic (secular) and theistic (religious) versions of existentialism developed over time. On the secular side, Jean-Paul Sartre, Albert Camus, Martin Heidegger and Karl Jaspers each contributed to the development of this philosophy. Sartre, a French philosopher, held that "...in the area of reason everything is absurd, but a person can authenticate himself by an act of the will . . . but, because as Sartre saw it, reason is separated from this authenticating, the will can act in any direction."[34] The German philosopher Martin Heidegger agreed with Sartre that reason had no role in finding answers to the questions of life. However, he offered a different perspective on how a person discovers meaning. Heidegger saw man as a "tragic figure in a finite world" and used the term "angst"[35] to describe man's experience in the world. Angst is not the same as fear. As Heidegger defined it, "fear has an object, while angst is the general feeling of anxiety one experiences in the universe."[36] Angst is what gives us a certainty of existence and forces us to make a decision or act. Through these decisions we discover meaning. (It's interesting to note how many of the reality TV programs involve some level of overcoming fear, i.e., *Fear Factor* or *Dog Eat Dog*.) Jaspers also centered his philosophy on the significance of individual experience. According to Frost, "He stressed the importance of the discrepancy between actual facts and the individual's interpretation of those facts. To Jaspers, truth is subjective, to a large extent non-rational, and constantly being reinterpreted by the individual."[37] Starting with Kant and continuing with Hegel and Kierkegaard, man's understanding of what we can know and how we can know changed dramatically. Existentialism had captivated the secular mind, but it also took ground in religious thinking.

Historically, the Bible had been viewed through the lens of the thesis/antithesis principle and **was accepted as the Word of God.** This is known as the fundamental position. Then as Enlightenment and deistic ideas were mingled with theology, a liberal position was developed. This view said **the Bible *is not* the Word of God.** A third view came about as a result of the work of the German theologian, Karl Barth. This idea, called Neo-Orthodoxy fuses existential thought with theology and states that **the Bible *becomes* the Word of God.** In other words, the Bible reports that revelation occurred and it could occur again. As a person experiences it, **the Bible *may become the Word of God,*** or it may not.

As you can imagine, these conflicting views of Scripture created waves of change throughout the West and the Christian world. But at the center of this debate were the issues with which man has struggled since the pre-Socratics. What can we really know and by what means? Is what we can know fixed or changing? What role do faith and reason have in helping us find answers?

Influenced by the thinkers we've reviewed, modern man in the West arrived at new answers to the key questions mentioned in the preceding paragraph. The answers were: trust in reason, put faith in science and progress, and be optimistic about the type of world humans can create. As a result, man also developed a new perspective on the future. In his eyes, a new and better world was on the horizon. Medicine, science, and technology will help society get there. We have ideals, but they do not exist objectively and we do not receive them from God. *We* establish them ourselves systematically and pragmatically. Man is fully capable of handling all of life...of setting his own course. God? He is diminished, dismissed, or even denied when it comes to everyday life.

Things such as world wars, famine, and increased crime caused modern man to become disillusioned with the world around him. Many no longer believed that reason and systematic thinking were enough to create a better world. Institutions such as governments and churches could not be trusted as they had been. The individual, experience, and choice became most important as man continued to attempt to find meaning in life and agreement about what is true. New definitions were being written for every aspect of life as individuals struggled to "find themselves." This transition in thinking and approach to life ushered in a new period of history in the West that thinkers have called the Postmodern era.

This Postmodern era is the period in which we currently live as we witness the full bloom of thinking that began hundreds of years ago. "According to post-moderns, truth is not merely a quality of statements that ascribe properties to the world. Nor should truth be limited to what can be verified by reason and the empirical scientific method. Instead post-moderns are convinced that there are ways of knowing in addition to reason such as through the emotions or intuition."[38]

Allan Bloom, author of *The Closing of the American Mind*[39], suggests that almost every student entering the university claims to believe that truth is relative, especially as it relates to morals. This denial of objective, universal, absolute truth lies at the heart of postmodernism, according to Bloom.

By understanding this mindset, you can recognize why postmodern is also sometimes called post-Christian, because the presuppositions about truth and knowing of a Christian worldview and a postmodern worldview stand in sharp contrast to one another. In the article titled, *"What is Postmodernism?"*, Bob Francis gives us a helpful explanation of how these views are different and the subsequent conflict that can result.

> *First according to postmodernism, culture shapes the person. In other words social forces like language, values and relationships mold human thought. People do what they do because their culture made them who they are. The natural result? An attitude of "It's not my fault," and a tendency to do whatever one pleases.*
>
> *Christians worry that this results in the breakdown of society, but the greatest problem, according to the postmodernist, is oppression. Because culture shapes the person, the dominant group way of thinking—such as the Judeo-Christian heritage—tends to*

force those who differ to the margins of society. Postmodernists seek to equalize these relationships, giving "marginalized" groups the power to overcome oppression and live as they choose.

The desire to give everyone a voice has led to political correctness and tolerance. It's OK to criticize the dominant group, such as Christianity, because this is part of the process of taking them out of power, but to criticize the "oppressed" group is bad, for it reinforces the problem.

Thus Christianity is viewed as particularly threatening; for it asserts that some beliefs are true and others false, thus repressing those who don't agree.

The second postmodern theme involves the acquisition of knowledge. Knowledge about the world is not discovered, but "constructed." Our perception of reality is colored by our culture. Trapped in our own subjectivity, we cannot perceive the external world as it really is. Since we've been culturally programmed, we never "discover" anything; rather we construct knowledge— essentially making it up as we go.

To know anything objectively would require people to transcend their cultural programming and that according to postmodernists is impossible. Actually, there's a sliver of truth in this. Unfortunately postmodernists make it an absolute. Rather than viewing the Bible as the only way to see life objectively, apart from cultural programming, they view the Bible as just another social construct, reflecting the "absolutist religious views" of people living 2,000 years ago. Those who believe in it are often labeled intolerant and close minded.

The third postmodern theme flows logically from the first two. Truth is relative, and each group or individual decides for themselves what is true. What is true or right for one person or group isn't necessarily true or right for another. Something is not believed because it is true, they say, rather it is true because it is believed. For example there is nothing "right" about monogamous heterosexual marriage apart from cultural conventions and traditions. And there is nothing "wrong" with homosexuality other than cultural prejudice. There exist no objective criteria or authority for moral judgment.[40]

As we have read, time has given us various men offering different answers and constructing diverse philosophies, but all struggled to answer the same questions. How do we know? What can we know? These questions have been and continue to be the starting point for understanding the formation of a worldview. In subsequent chapters, we will wrestle with other critical questions such as the nature of the universe, the existence of good and evil, fate versus free will, plus others. However, it's important to remember that a person's view of truth and knowing establishes the foundation for how he will answer the other key questions that form a worldview.

> *The prevalent view today in academic circles at least tends to place philosophical opinions and religious beliefs on the side of taste rather than on the side of truth. This has not always been regnant view, nor is it necessarily the correct one.*[41]
>
> Mortimer Adler
> *Six Great Ideas*

DISCUSSION QUESTIONS

1) What role did reason play during the Age of Enlightenment?

2) Who was Immanuel Kant? When did he live? And for what is he known?

3) Who was George W. F. Hegel? When did he live? Explain his dialectic system.

4) What did Francis Schaeffer mean by the statement: *"One cannot understand modern man in philosophy, in the other disciplines, in morals, in political thought, without understanding that Hegel has won."*

5) Who was Sören Kierkegaard? When did he live and for what is he best known?

6) Describe Kierkegaard's "leap of faith" and its effects upon Christianity.

7) Identify and define the three views of the Bible that exist because of these philosophical changes.

8) How does a postmodern view of truth and knowing affect evangelism? Morality? Education?

9) How does a person's view of how and what we can know affect what is acceptable and appropriate in culture?

4

———•◆•———

THE NATURE OF THE UNIVERSE

*The world in which you and I live was here long before us.
How did it come to be? Was it created or has it existed forever?
Who or what made it, and how was it made? Are the trees, stars,
men and women really "there," or are they mere creations of our
minds or of the mind of God? How came this universe to be and
what is it made of?*

S. E. Frost
Basic Teachings of the Great Philosophers[42]

It is a rare person who can gaze upon the stars and not wonder,
"Where did all this come from?" For as long as mankind has
existed, he has sought to come up with some account for how the
world began…and how it might end. In addition, mankind has tried
to explain the existence and relationship of the material (physical)
and immaterial (metaphysical or spiritual) worlds. This field of study
is known as cosmology and can be defined as the study of the history,
structure, and dynamics of the universe.[43]

How Did All This Begin?

If you survey thinkers' attempts to explain the origin of the
universe, you will find that there are numerous and varied narratives.
However, there are generally four answers given to the question,
"How did the world begin?" They are:

1. It was created.
2. It happened by chance.
3. It has always been this way or is eternal.
4. It's all an illusion.

S. E. Frost points out that this question of origins is the place where most philosophy begins.

> *The earliest philosophers, the Greeks, were greatly interested in this problem of the nature of the universe. Indeed, it was the first problem they attacked. Just as children break open their toys to discover how they are made, these philosophers of the childhood of the human race sought to break apart the universe in their minds, and to penetrate the mystery of the making of all found in it.*[44]

Starting with the pre-Socratics, Greek thinkers offered various theories about the beginning and formation of the world. For the most part, they suggested the world was made of tiny atoms that were all alike. Consequently, they are often referred to as Atomists. These atoms combined in different ways and in various numbers to compose the "stuff" that makes up the universe. They were eternal and could not change, although it was difficult for thinkers to reach consensus on how the atoms and "stuff" came into existence. Most of their theories focused on describing aspects of the material or seen world. Plato, on the other hand, introduced a theory that described the world in two realms or layers (see Truth and Knowing–Part 1). In formulating his theory about the nature of the universe, Plato also offered an explanation on how things came into existence.

> *For Plato, the world which we see, touch and experience through our senses is not real, but a copy world. In it we find things changing, coming and going and in great abundance. It is a world*

of many mistakes, deformities, evils. It exists and we experience it every day. But it is not real.

There is, however, a real world in which are to be found the true things of which all that we experience are mere copies. He called this the world of "ideas." Here is to be found the ideal tree of which all trees we see are copies, the ideal house, and ideas of all other objects in the universe. These are perfect, do not change in any way, never fade or die, but remain forever.

In one of Plato's famous Dialogues, the Timaeus, he tells us how the world of our senses was created. There was an "architect," the "Demiurge," who brought the ideal world and matter together to produce a statue. This "Demiurge" had perfect ideas of everything and he had a great mass of matter. Plato never tells us where the Demiurge, ideas or matter came from originally. They were just there when things began.[45]

It's worth noting that Plato recognized that there was a design to the world, which led him to believe there must be a designer, whom he called the *Demiurge*. However, he was not able to offer any details about how the architect or the material he used came to be.

Plato's student, Aristotle, also offered a theory on the origin of the universe. His thinking attempted to mediate between the Atomists and Plato. S. E. Frost summarizes Aristotle's thinking below:

If we wish to understand the universe, then we may think of it in terms of a sculpture producing a statue. But while in the case of Plato, the sculptor is independent, free from his marble, in the case of Aristotle, he is dependent on the marble. His idea of the perfect statue is actually in the marble, a form which the marble seeks to realize.

It is clear from what we have already said that Aristotle's world is not a purely mechanical something. It is not a mere mass of units or atoms moving about and forming objects, as the Atomists taught. Rather it is characterized by purposes which matter seeks to realize. There is striving in the universe, a seeking to become.

We call such a world "teleological," not a world of mere chance but one of purpose.

If the acorn seeks to become an oak tree and the oak tree seeks to become a piece of furniture, where does the process stop? Is everything seeking to become something else, and there is no end to the chain? Aristotle believed that there was an end. This he thought of as the first cause or the "unmoved mover." [46]

Like Plato before him, Aristotle offered an explanation of the world and included a starting point called the "unmoved mover." However, the unmoved mover was not personal or knowable, just simply a first cause.

The next most significant thinker following Aristotle was Epicurus. He taught that the world had no original designer or cause, but instead he believed the world came into existence by chance. His followers believed the world was composed of atoms that initially fell in a straight line from space. However, these atoms have the power to swerve, and as some went left and some right, bodies of the universe were formed. These atoms can neither be divided nor destroyed and have existed forever; therefore, the universe will continue on like this indefinitely.

Other philosophers offered derivations on these themes to explain the universe. However, it was the Jewish, and then Christian thinkers, who explained the origin of the universe as being created "ex nihilo," by a personal, knowable God. "Ex nihilo," means "from nothing" so God is the causeless First Cause. Everything that is created was first conceived of in His mind and then came about because He spoke it into existence. A. W. Tozer describes this act as follows, "In the beginning He spoke to nothing, and it became something. Chaos heard it and became order; darkness heard it and became light. And God said. . . and it was so."[47] (Genesis 1:9) This idea of ex nihilo was important in distinguishing a Christian explanation from the Greeks. For although many key Greek philosophers agreed that there had to be a creator, Christians identify who the creator is and how He made all things.

Through the Middle Ages, the Christian response to the question "How did it all begin?" was the widely accepted answer in the West. Then as we moved through the Renaissance and Enlightenment, religious traditions and philosophical musings were diminished or dismissed. Scientific explanations were fast becoming the only acceptable option. Answers influenced by upper story thinking were rejected as untrustworthy fables, and everything was now explained from a lower story point of view. Up until this point, the theologian or philosopher was the one who gave cosmological answers, but now it was the scientist. (In fact, prior to this shift, cosmology was often thought to be the realm of the philosopher, but now it was the realm of the scientist.)

As a result, man continued to attempt to answer the question of origin, by developing new hypotheses, which didn't include theological explanations. The most widely publicized premise was the big bang theory. Although many people may think this idea has been around for a long time, it was first proposed in 1927 by a Belgian priest named George LeMaitre.[48] He suggested that somewhere between 10 and 20 billion years ago, the universe began with the explosion of one primeval atom. This cataclysmic explosion sent matter hurtling through space in all directions. As these atoms crashed together, galaxies and all other matter was formed, and life began. This certainly has been the most widely accepted theory since the early 1960s and is often thought of as a new discovery. It is interesting to compare the big bang with the thoughts of Epicurus, who lived around 300 BC. There are a number of similarities between these explanations, which bring to mind the words of Solomon who wrote in Ecclesiastes, "There is nothing new under the sun." One other point worth noting is that the big bang does not give an explanation for how that first atom appeared. It's just assumed it was there. That's why, though the big bang is widely received, it is not completely provable; therefore, it still leaves a number of unanswered questions.

Along with the big bang, scientists have more recently introduced another theory called "Intelligent Design." This idea recognizes that the universe is not random, but gives evidence of design and order. However, it stops short of identifying a Designer. It simply states that if you observe the universe, it appears there's a plan and that some intelligence was applied to the way the universe works. However, not all scientists have embraced this view, and so the debate rages on. But as thinkers wrestle with how the universe began, they are also faced with the question, "What Is the Nature Of the Universe?" In other words, what is the existence of and relationship between the material (physical) and immaterial (metaphysical) worlds? That's where we will turn our attention to next.

What Is the Nature Of the Universe?

As with the origin of the universe, answers to the question, "What Is the Nature Of the Universe?" are varied. However, the key question that is often asked is "What is real?" This question helps determine what is important. Generally, there are four different views about the nature of the world.

1. **There are two realities, material and non-material**. Both are knowable and important and they are distinct from one another.

2. **There are two realities, material and non-material.** Both are knowable and important, but they are <u>not</u> distinct from one another.

3. **There is only one reality, non-material.** Everything else including matter is a projection of the mind and merely an idea.

4. **There is only one reality, material.** There is no unseen world. What we can see and experience through our senses is what's real.

We will look at each of these in more detail, but it is worth calling to mind again how the major presuppositions impacting worldview affect each other. For certain, what a person believes about "How we know?" and "What we can know?" will affect how he or she sees the nature of the universe. So even though we are examining these issues independently, we must never forget that they exist in our minds as interrelated ideas. How we view any one of these issues affects how we see the others (see Figure 9). Keeping that in mind, let's examine the four major thoughts about the nature of the universe.

How Worldview Is Formed

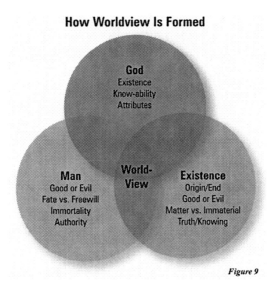

Figure 9

The first idea is that there are two realities, material and non-material. This view was the widely accepted explanation about the nature of the universe from the pre-Socratics through the Renaissance. Although there was much debate about our ability to know each realm and its relevant importance, there was little debate about the existence of each world. A Christian worldview recognizes the idea that there are two realities. Both of them are created by God and both are good. Both realms are also knowable and important. However, this is not the way people have attempted to explain the nature of the universe.

A second position that developed is the idea that there are two realities, but they are not distinct from one another. Take Bernard Spinoza, for example. He lived in the mid-1600's and taught that the world is not made of two substances, such as ideas and matter, but rather one substance, which he called God. The universe is thus made up of "God-infused" parts which form the whole. The trees, the rocks, the sky, man, and animals are all a part of God, and in actuality are God. According to Spinoza, God is the universe and the universe is God. Now if this all sounds strangely familiar, it should. It is pantheism and it's always been one of the ideas man trots out to explain the nature of the universe. It is important to recognize this idea stands in conflict with a Christian worldview, which says that God is distinct from His creation. He is not made of parts, but exists independent of His creation.

A third idea that gained acceptance was that there was only one reality and it is non-material. For example, Johann Fichte, who lived from 1768 to 1814, and helped found the University of Berlin, set forth the idea that there is no matter in the universe. Everything, according to Fichte, is either mind or spirit or idea. The world to us only *seems* to be material, but in reality is only mind and spirit. In other words, all that we experience in the material realm is actually just our perception and only exists as we perceive it in our own minds. Although, to many this position may seem absurd, it's interesting to note that throughout history man has always suggested this possibility to explain existence.

A fourth explanation for the nature of the universe is that there is just one reality and it is material. For the most part, this idea didn't gain support until after the Enlightenment because this belief of a material-only world denies the existence of an upper story or immaterial world. It also typically rejects the existence of God or any spiritual reality, which were both positions that found wide acceptance post-Enlightenment. Consequently, this view also tends to see the world or existence as mechanical in nature and elevates man and science above all else. In addition, this view of reality helps foster the development of hedonism, materialism, and consumerism that have been dominant worldviews in the West over the past sixty years.

How Will It All End?

Now that we've considered how the world began and what is the nature of the world as we know it, there is still one nagging question left to address, "How will all this end?" Theories have varied, but generally there are four explanations offered.

1. It never ends, but just continues indefinitely.
2. It does end eventually, because it simply runs out of energy or decays.
3. There is a cataclysmic end with no clear future.
4. There is a cataclysmic end that ushers in a new age.

Let's look at each of these. First, there is the idea that the world never ends, but continues on indefinitely. This theory is tied to the view that the world has always existed this way and will never change. The difficulty with accepting this position is that the world around us is changing all the time. True, there are cycles and seasons of time, but change and decay are everywhere. In addition, there seems to be something teleological about the nature of man. In other words, there seems to be a sense that we are moving toward something. "This" is not all there is. In fact, the other three explanations all agree an end is inevitable. They just don't agree on how it will happen and what happens next.

One theory is that the universe ends but not because of some cataclysmic event. In fact, just a couple of years ago, *Time* ran a cover story titled, *"How The Universe Will End."*[49] In the lead article, an explanation and timeline shows how the universe will eventually decay into nothingness. Accepting this theory on how it all ends, however, requires you to accept their theory on how it all began, which they say is the big bang. According to the article, the big bang took place about 15 billion years ago. From that point forward, the universe has been expanding and will continue to expand until a period about 10 trillion trillion trillion years after the big bang. Then, we will enter a period called the degenerate era where, "planets will detach from stars; stars and planets evaporate from galaxies. Most of the ordinary matter in the universe *will be* locked up in degenerate stellar remnants… eventually, over spans of time greatly exceeding the current age of the universe, the protons themselves decay." Following that period is the Black Hole era. This age extends to "10,000 trillion trillion trillion trillion trillion trillion trillion trillion years after the Big Bang. The only large objects remaining are black holes, which eventually evaporate into photons and other types of radiation." Then *Time* suggests that in the final phase, which is called the dark era, only waste products will remain and "from here into the infinite future, the universe remains cold, dark and dismal." Not a very optimistic picture of the future, but it is difficult to imagine even the possibility of knowing something with surety so astronomically far ahead in time. This view is a rather recent development based on data gathered in just the past five years.

A more widely accepted premise is that there will be a cataclysmic end, but with no clear future. Think about it. Many films have depicted some meteor, volcano, alien invasion, robots, or over-heated core of the earth threatening to end life as we know it. They all tell us the end is coming but with no explanation of why or what will happen next. The general idea is that somehow, some part of the earth or universe has left its safe bounds and has run amok. Meteors hurtling toward earth! Aliens coming to destroy us! There are any number of threats to our existence, yet there is a common theme to these stories. Man must do something to save himself. Man must act or be doomed. Man is the key player and survival is dependent on his ingenuity and overcoming his fears and limits.

In contrast, the Christian worldview agrees that there will be a type of cataclysmic end, but it's really not an end. It's a glorious beginning. The key figure in the story is not man, but the Lord Jesus Christ. In Chapter 20 of the book of Revelation, it says:

> *When the thousand years are ended, Satan will be released from his prison and will come out to deceive the nations at the four corners of the earth, Gog and Magog, in order to gather them for battle; they are as numerous as the sands of the sea. They marched up over the breadth of the earth and surrounded the camp of the saints and the beloved city. And fire came down from heaven and consumed them. And the devil who had deceived them was thrown into the lake of fire and sulfur, where the beast and the false*

prophet were, and they will be tormented day and night forever and ever.[50]

Following fire coming down from heaven to consume the enemies of God, judgment comes. Revelation goes on to tell us that Jesus Christ will sit on the Great White Throne to judge the dead. At that time, death and Hades and all those whose names are not written in the book of life will be thrown into the lake of fire. But that is not the end. In contrast to most other cataclysmic narratives that leave the earth as a smoldering, ashen ember, the Bible tells us there will be a rebirth or renovation of all things (Matt 10:28, Acts 3:21). In fact, the end as we know it is really the fulfillment or consummation of a plan. The end comes to pass not because something in the mechanized universe has gone awry as some cataclysmic stories would lead you to believe. Nor is mankind the victim of an earth or creation gone haywire. On the contrary, mankind in proper relationship with God is actually the recipient of a wonderful, beautiful, new dwelling place. Once again, Revelation gives us the details.

Then I saw a new heaven and a new earth; for the first heaven and the first earth had passed away, and the sea was no more. And I saw the holy city, the new Jerusalem, coming down out of heaven from God, prepared as a bride adorned for her husband. And I heard a loud voice from the throne saying, "See, the home of God is among mortals. He will dwell with them as their God; they will be his peoples, and God himself will be with them; he will wipe every tear from their eyes. Death will be no more; mourning and crying and pain will be no more, for the first things have passed away." And the one who was seated on the throne said, "See, I am making all things new." Also he said, "Write this, for these words are trustworthy and true." Then he said to me, "It is done! I am the Alpha and the Omega, the beginning and the end. To the thirsty I will give water as a gift from the spring of the water of life. Those

*who conquer will inherit these things, and I will be their God and
they will be my children."*[51]

What an amazing picture. A new heaven. A new earth. A new
Jerusalem. Jesus Christ seated on the throne quenching the thirst of
those who dwell there. Then, the Apostle John adds this:

> *I saw no temple in the city, for its temple is the Lord God the
> Almighty and the Lamb. And the city has no need of sun or moon
> to shine on it, for the glory of God is its light, and its lamp is the
> Lamb. The nations will walk by its light, and the kings of the
> earth will bring their glory into it. Its gates will never be shut by
> day—and there will be no night there.*[52]

The contrast here is significant. Whereas the other explanations
of how things end suggest there is nothing to look forward to, a
Christian worldview tells us the best is yet to come. Where the
others suggest the future holds nothing good, the Christian
worldview tells us there's something amazing ahead. Where the
others tell us the future is either in the hands of or out of the control
of man, a Christian worldview tells us it actually lies in the finished
work of Jesus Christ. Where the others leave us with a sense of
uncertainty or dread, a Christian worldview gives us hope and a
sense of anticipation.

In addition, there is another key difference between a Christian
worldview and the other options: judgment. The Bible tells us in
Hebrews 9:27, "And just as it is appointed for men to die once, then
comes judgment."[53] So how we live now and the choices we make
matter, because at some point we will be judged for them. All the
other narratives do not demand any accountability for now because
it won't matter then. But a Christian view of the end has very real

and important present implications. That's something we never want
to forget.

> *Some say the world will end in fire*
> *Some say in ice*
> *From what I've tasted of desire*
> *I hold with those who favor fire.*

> Robert Frost[54]

DISCUSSION QUESTIONS

1) What are the major answers to the question, "What is the origin of the universe?" Give examples of each.

2) What are some of the implications of the viewpoints listed above with respect to morals? Community? Personal meaning? Current events?

3) How does a Christian explain the relationship and integration of the material (visible) and immaterial (invisible) worlds? How does this differ with other explanations of the material (visible) and immaterial (invisible) worlds?

4) What are the major answers to the question, "What is the end of the universe?" Give examples of each.

5) Why does it matter what a person believes about the end of the universe?

6) What do you think most people around you believe concerning their personal destiny?

7) How can you engage non-Christians in meaningful conversations about these topics?

5

———◆·◆———

MAN'S PLACE IN THE UNIVERSE

When I consider Thy heavens, the work of Thy fingers, the moon and the stars which Thou hast ordained; what is man, that Thou dost take thought of him? And the son of man that Thou dost care for him? Yet Thou hast made him a little lower than the God, and dost crown him with glory and majesty! Thou dost make him to rule over the works of Thy hands; Thou hast put all things under his feet, all sheep and oxen and also the beasts of the field, the birds of the heavens, the fish of the sea, whatever passes through the paths of the sea.

Psalm 8:3-8 NASB[55]

A long with wondering where the universe came from and how it all will end, man has also struggled with the issue of his place in creation. Is man the pinnacle of creation as King David expressed in Psalm 8? Or has man simply evolved by chance over millions of years from a common ancestor of the gorilla or chimpanzee? By chance, man, like the rest of the physical world, has always existed; no creation; no evolution; just always here. Or perhaps, man is simply a projection of the universal mind and not distinct in any way from a rock, a tree, a dog, a star or God.

This question of man's beginning is a significant one. In most cases, what a person believes about the origin of man is influenced by his views on other matters such as the nature of the universe and the existence of God. For example, if a person holds to the big bang theory, it would be less likely that he or she would see man as created in the image of God. (Although in our pluralistic culture, a person is often free to create a personal blend of theories to answer the big questions—even if the answers are contradictory.) In our day, opinions abound about man's origin, but most of the focus in the West over the past eight decades have centered on the debate between evolution and creation. The famous Scopes Monkey trial in 1925 helped bring this conflict to the forefront. In this landmark case, John Scopes was charged with violating a Tennessee law that prohibited the teaching of Darwin's theory of evolution in a public classroom. Darwin's theory simply states that natural selection and environmental factors combine to explain the diversity we see on earth, rather than the purposeful plan and design of God. The result is that one species can—over time—become another species. For example, monkeys become a man or a fish becomes a bird. For obvious reasons, those who believe that man was created by God reject Darwin's theory, because this idea eliminates the activity of God in the formation and design of the earth's inhabitants, including man. Furthermore, it elevates chance as a supreme force in the universe.

Since the 1920s evolution has arguably been the most widely accepted and taught view in the United States. In fact, just a couple of years ago, *Time* ran a cover story titled, *"How Apes Became Human."* The lead article reported on the discovery of new fossils in Ethiopia that seemed to give further evidence to support the theory of evolution. In the same article however, the writer states:

> *While this view of human evolution has generally been accepted by scientists for decades, no one has been able to say precisely when the first evolutionary step on the road to humanity has happened, nor what might have triggered it.*[56]

So while evolution has been taught as being fully explained or validated by science, it is not.

What Is Man's Place?

The discussion about man's origin is one that will likely continue for some time, but day-to-day the more burning issue for most people is, "What is man's place in the universe?" In other words, what role and opportunity does man have in determining his purpose and destiny? Philosophers have considered this question for thousands of years, but generally have arrived at four possibilities to explain man's place in the cosmos. They are:

1. Man is fated and subject to the forces of the universe.
2. Man is the center of the universe and is the full determinant of his destiny.
3. Man is subject to chance and there is nothing sure, predictable or controllable.
4. Man is created by God with purpose and intentionality.

Let's examine each of these. First, man is fated and subject to the universe. Early Greek thinking reflected this view. In fact, Greek mythology included three beings called the Fates. According to legend, these Fates predated the gods and had the responsibility and power to determine a man's destiny and assign him to be good or evil. One Fate determined how long a person lived. A second chose a person's lot in life and length of years. A third actually "snipped the thread of life" that fixed the time of death.

However, it didn't take long for the Greeks to abandon this view and declare man as the center of the universe. Protagoras, who lived in the fifth century B.C., set forth that, "man is the measure of all things." In other words, man is free to determine his own destiny and shape the universe, or as S. E. Frost observes, "...at least that part which was of most importance to him."[57] Man is now the master, not the subject.

These contrasting ideas, man as fated and man at the center, stand as two ends of a continuum (see Figure 10) and always seem to reappear in slightly different forms. Modern man rejects the mythological idea of the Fates but at times has suggested the universe is a mechanized entity of which man is simply a cog in the machine. For example, Liebnitz, the German philosopher (1646-1716), saw the world as completely mechanical. Therefore, to him, man and all of nature is subject to law, order, and uniformity.

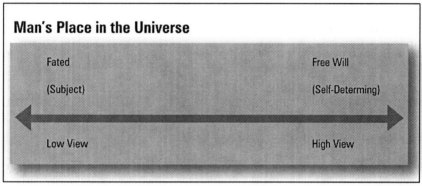

Man's Place in the Universe

Fated   Free Will

(Subject)   (Self-Determing)

Low View   High View

Figure 10

More often though the idea that man is at the center of the universe is the view that governs popular thought. Starting with the Renaissance, which placed man as the reference point for all things, the idea that man is in control has dominated thinking in the West for the past 800 years. S. E. Frost compares this development to the waking and unleashing of a fettered giant and then makes this observation:

Man dared to assert his ability to control the world, to know the innermost secrets and by the power of his intellect master its ways and turn them to his desires. ...The spirit of man had caught a faint glimpse of the future and would not be denied entrance into the Promised Land. Never again would man be satisfied to bow in utter subjection to the powers of the universe. He would stand erect and demand the right to challenge the universe and master its secrets. This was indeed a new day for man and the birth of a new conception of man's place in the universe.[58]

Some might argue that this idea of man at the center, which Frost suggests was birthed in the Renaissance, was merely adopted from Protagoras. Yet no matter when you believe it originated, this suggestion of man as the measure was even more fully embraced by Enlightenment philosophers. Men like Jean Jacques Rousseau and Immanuel Kant rejected the idea that man was merely part of a mechanized world and emphasized freedom. Fichte, another key Enlightenment thinker also made freedom a focus of all his writings. According to Fichte, man is "... fundamentally a free agent, not a mere link in a predetermined chain of material events. Self-determining activity is the supreme characteristic of man."[59]

Many other post-Enlightenment thinkers have also held on to this idea. For example, men like John Dewey (1859-1952), who had a profound influence on the American education system, also saw man as the measure of the universe. The point is, even though modern life and technology have given man a greater sense that he is in control, the idea that the universe is at his command is not a recent development.

As man has wrestled with the question of his place in the universe, two other options have presented themselves. The first is that neither position that we have already considered is true. Man is neither subject to the universe nor in control. Instead man is simply subject to chance. There is nothing sure, predictable, or controllable in this life. This idea is similar to being fated in that it takes a pessimistic view of man's position, but it is different in that there is no master plan working out. Life and existence are random. You might get something good. You might get something bad. You just don't know. You just have to live life and see what happens.

Existential thinkers tend to see life this way and quite often this view shows up in our entertainment. Take for example, the lovable movie character Forest Gump, played by Tom Hanks. He would certainly not be considered an intellectual, but Gump gives us an excellent summation of this philosophy, when he says repeatedly, "Momma always said life is like a box of chocolates. You never know what you're gonna get." What is Gump saying? Nothing is for sure. Just pick out something to do. If it's distasteful, try something else. Some of it will be good. Some of it will be bad. You can't really know for sure.

The final viewpoint to consider stands in contrast to the idea that life is random. It is the idea that man is created by God with purpose and destiny but can also make choices. This has been a predominantly Christian view and on the continuum between fate and free will, it sits clearly in the middle (see Figure 11). Man, made in the image of God, has a design and intent to his life so there is an element of "fated-ness." Yet there is also some capacity for choice, so "willing-ness" is also present. To what degree each of these operates in a person's life has been the subject of much debate over the years. Tension has been created as people try to reconcile calling and predestination with freedom to choose; God's sovereignty and omnipotence with man's will. Yet, despite the friction that exists, this view does place man in a position of dignity. He has power but is not limitless. He is important but not supreme. He has a destiny but can choose.

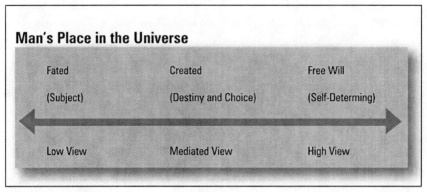

Figure 11

Consequences and Authority

In addition to acknowledging these different views, it's also important to recognize the consequences of each position and the authority that is established in a person's life as a result. For example, a fated view, which holds that man has no choice or control, often leads to an apathetic or cynical outlook on life. In other words, it doesn't really matter what you do because whatever is supposed to happen will happen anyway. That's why people who have this perspective often look to simple social conventions or the most utilitarian option when making decisions.

In contrast, a view that puts man at the center leads him to believe that he is in control of everything. There is an unwavering confidence in man's ability and a conviction that all choices are possible. Man need not trust anyone or anything more than himself. As a result, majority opinion, self-government, and democracy are held in highest regard when it comes to decision making and governing people's affairs.

But the person who sees himself created for a purpose by God views life from a much different vantage point. There is an intentionality and accountability to living. The authority in his life is not an impersonal or unfriendly universe or his own desires and ambitions. The authority in his life is a just God and His Word.

Why Is this Issue of Authority Important?

This question of authority is not an issue that people usually speak about or even overtly identify. However, **the key point is that every person has some authority in his life**—whether he acknowledges it or not. Usually, people's choices and decisions indicate what *the* personal authority is in their life. It can be anything from the need to be popular, a desire for money or recognition, a fear of failure, or a conviction to please God. It can also change over time in a person's life. However, we are all ruled by something or someone when making decisions.

Furthermore, it's important to remember that personal authority does not develop or exist independently. Other factors, such as a person's conception of truth or view of God, create the foundation on which authority is built and influence other presuppositions that are part of his or her worldview. Understanding this can be very helpful as we interact with people, because in some cases, we can back into a person's worldview by observing the personal authority in his life. Conversely, if we understand the authority in people's lives, we can anticipate where their worldview might lead them. As you interact with people every day, you will find that many of the challenges and frustrations you face stem from the fact that everyone operates from different spheres of authority, which is really a function of their worldview. It also helps to explain why people make decisions that don't seem to make sense to us.

But grappling with the question of our place in the universe isn't the only big question we have to answer. At some point, we must all decide what happens to us when we die. Is there life after death, and if so, what will it be like? That is the issue we'll consider in the next chapter.

> *What a piece of work is man, how noble in reason, how infinite in faculties. In form and moving, how express and admirable in action, how like an angel in apprehension, how like a god? The beauty of the world; the paragon of animals; and yet to me what is this quintessence of dust? Man delights not me—not woman either...*
>
> Shakespeare. Hamlet..[60]

DISCUSSION QUESTIONS

1) What are the four primary answers that thinkers have given to the question, "What is man's place in the universe?"

2) Where do you see examples of those ideas expressed in culture today?

3) What are some of the personal consequences and social ramifications of each position?

4) What views of man do you encounter among the people you interact with everyday?

5) Typically, there is a connection between one's understanding of man's place in the universe and his view of authority. Do you see any disconnect in the church between the view of man and authority?

6) If so, what are the ramifications?

7) What would you say to someone who makes the statement, "Man is completely free"?

6

THE SOUL AND IMMORTALITY

There are, aren't there, only three things we can do about death: to desire it, to fear it, or to ignore it.

C. S. Lewis
Letters to an American Lady[61]

Tomorrow, and tomorrow, and tomorrow
Creeps in this petty pace from day to day
To the last syllable of recorded time;
And all our yesterdays have lighted fools
The way to dusty death. Out, out brief candle!
Life's but a walking shadow, a poor player,
That struts and frets his hour upon the stage,
And then is heard no more: it is a tale
Told by an idiot, full of sound and fury,
Signifying nothing.

William Shakespeare
Macbeth[62]

In William Shakespeare's play, *Macbeth,* the main character offers this eloquent perspective on life and death and draws our attention to the fact that we all face the undeniable, unavoidable reality of death. In most cases, this new realization often leads us to ask the question, "What happens when I die?"

It's clear to anyone who attends a funeral that death is real. But its inevitability also causes us to wonder, "Does man have a soul?"

And if he does have a soul, what is its nature? S. E. Frost suggests that most people would say man does have a soul. In his book, *Basic Teachings of the Great Philosophers*, he makes this observation:

> *Throughout the history of mankind there has persisted a conviction, sometimes dim and at other times very vivid, that death cannot be the end, that the grave is not a victory of man's foes, that death does not inflict a cosmic sting. In every age there have been millions firm in the belief that what is truest in humanity persists in some form or state after death.*[63]

Yet, as we will see, many modern thinkers disagree with Frost's statement and have even suggested that, "the doctrine of the soul may be definitely harmful since it carries with it a load of tradition which weights man down...."[64]

Is man more than just a body? Does he have a soul? And if he does, what is the soul made of and what happens to it at death? These questions have been, and continue to be, the subject of much discussion and theorizing. But for now, let's accept the idea that man has a soul.

The first question we must consider is the composition of the soul. Is it immaterial or material? Most who believe in the soul see it as an immaterial or spirit-like part of human beings. It exists apart from the body. But is the soul something unique to man? Is that what makes us human? Or are humans just one of the living organisms that have a soul?

Views of the Soul

Early man likely came to accept the idea that we had souls because through his dreams, he had a sense of going places, seeing and doing things even though his body never moved. But if he had a soul, what about the other living things around him? The trees? The river? They had life in them, so in most cases, he concluded they must have a soul as well. But that raised another question? Where did souls come from and what happens to them once the body is destroyed? As you can imagine, early Greek thinkers could not let this question lie unexamined.

Two Early Explanations of the Soul

Hellenistic thinkers offered two very different ideas about the soul. First was the idea that the soul was immaterial, created, and eternal. Plato championed this view. According to him, the Demiurge gave souls to everything from planets to individuals. The individual souls were eternal and existed before they took up residence in the body. But for Plato, indwelling the body was like a prison for the soul. The goal of the soul was to free itself so that it may see truth more clearly as it did in its pre-embodied existence. This interpretation of the soul would make sense to Plato if you recall his views of the upper and lower stories and the world of ideas being superior to the material world.

In addition, Plato made a strong case for the immortality of the soul. For him, the soul was the most basic element of life and, therefore would always remain life. It could not become non-life, no more than non-life can become life. Life and non-life were eternal, unchanging states; and therefore, the soul being life was immortal.

In contrast to Plato, the Epicureans declared that the soul was material and disintegrated when the body died. If you remember, they were Atomists and viewed the world composed of atoms that collided and formed entities. The Atomists believed the only logical option was that the soul, which was made of atoms, re-scattered at death and went on to form some other entity. Eternal pre-existence and immortality of the soul, which were fundamental truths for Plato, were rejected by the Atomists. For them, the soul came to be when a person was formed and ceased to exist when the person died.

Early Christians did not believe either of these ideas were correct and proposed a third option. Governed by the truth of the Bible, men like Augustine established that man is a union of the soul, which is immaterial, and the body, which is material. The soul was given to man by God. Whether it existed before the body or came into being at conception was a matter of debate. However, Christian thinkers did agree that the soul lived forever and faced an eternal existence in heaven or hell based on the choices a person made in the body. How is that eternal destiny determined? What role does man have in that final destination? Theologians have debated those issues for thousands of years without reaching consensus. Yet, they all agree man has a soul and is immortal.

To this point, we have considered three different views of the soul, which were dominant prior to the Renaissance. They are:

1. The soul is immaterial, created and eternal.
2. The soul is material and disintegrates when the body dies.
3. Man is a union of the soul, which is immaterial and given by God, and the material body.

Our desire here is neither to examine every idea conceived about the soul nor to fully trace the historical development and cultural influences that have impacted thinking about the soul. Rather, the intent is to identify the major viewpoints regarding the soul and then understand how each influences a person's view of life after death. With that in mind, there are two other ideas that warrant mention.

Other Ideas about the Soul

The first belief is that man has a soul, but it is not distinctly his. Rather his soul is part of a larger universal soul. This universal soul shows up in all living things, including man. The French philosopher, Rene Descartes (1596-1650) is an example of someone who held this view. According to Descartes,

> ....the soul is part of the whole, part of God or absolute substance. It cannot be thought of as disappearing, but continues as long as God continues. Death of the body is but a change, and the soul, being free of the body and never actually influenced by it, is not affected by its disintegration.[65]

Another philosopher who proposed similar ideas was Benedict Spinoza (1632-1677) who lived at roughly the same time as Descartes. Like Descartes, Spinoza taught that:

> ... Since God was the only substance, the soul could be nothing less than a mode of God. As such, it was identified with the spiritual side of the universe. Soul was perceived when one looked at substance from the side of the mind rather than from the side of body.
>
> Further, as a mode of the absolute substance, the soul could not be immortal in an individual sense, but it did have immortality as a mode of God which could not be destroyed any more than God could be destroyed.[66]

According to Spinoza, the soul is immortal, but not in a personal sense. To some degree, this idea is just pantheism dressed up in philosophical clothing. Furthermore, it could be argued that primitive man held similar views in his worship of trees and volcanoes, so these men were not actually proposing new ideas.

A second explanation of the soul that was widely accepted was the idea that we cannot know the soul exists for sure. Many credit the Enlightenment philosopher Immanuel Kant with first proposing this theory.

> *Kant held that the understanding cannot know anything but that which is experienced. However, reason can go beyond this and conceive of a world of which we can no actual experience. Thus it transcends, rises above experience, and gives transcendent principles. Reason gives man an idea of soul as the summation for all mental processes. Although we can never experience the soul, the idea of soul has value and therefore it is legitimate for us to think of it.*
>
> *Since there can be no knowledge without a knower, it is legitimate for us to conclude that there is such a thing as a soul, and act as if it existed. Although we cannot prove the existence of an immortal soul, we may act as though one existed since there is real value in so doing.*
>
> *Further the idea of the soul has ethical value. It is a result of the moral law and serves as a basis for moral life. But man cannot become absolutely good at any moment during his mortal existence. Consequently, this principle makes the immortality of the soul necessary so that the demands of the moral law may be met. During this endless time made necessary and possible, the human soul goes on and on to perfection, to a complete realization of the demands of the moral law.*[67]

Many who came after Kant followed the trajectory of his thought. As a result, most modern philosophers have completely abandoned the idea of the soul and individual immortality. August Comte (1798-1857), who is described as a philosopher from the Positivistic school of thought, believed concepts of soul and immortality were characteristics of an immature or childish phase in human development. According to Comte:

As man becomes more mature in his racial development, he recognizes that such beliefs are not exact, that they are mere wishes which cannot be proven or founded upon fact. Consequently, they must be abandoned.[68]

Philosophers from the Pragmatic school of thought shared similar convictions. Men like the American thinker William James (1842-1910) accepted that many people believe in the soul's existence and immortality. He even saw this thought as having some usefulness in man's moral life. However, he did not believe in the existence of the soul himself. John Dewey was more adamant in his view. He was "convinced that the doctrine of the soul may be definitely harmful since it carries a load of tradition which weights man down or causes him to give up altogether the attempt to understand experience...." [69]

These men and others like them believed that science was creating progress and moving human beings to a more highly evolved existence. However, to get to this new advanced state, mankind must shun ideas of the past and only trust in those things that can be validated by scientific inquiry. Since the soul and immortality are not provable, we really can't say they exist. So, to discuss them as though they are real is meaningless and foolish. In fact, most of these modern thinkers believed that science cannot validate most religious thoughts, so people must reject them. That's why for men like Comte and Dewey, religious ideas are immature thoughts of a lesser developed human. Soul and immortality are words with no meaning or even negative connotations.

What Happens When You Die?

To this point we've taken a considerable amount of time to focus on the soul, yet most people with whom you interact day-to-day probably don't talk much about it. They probably have an opinion about the soul, but rarely share it. They are more likely to tell you what they think happens to a person after death. This is something we all think about because deep down we all know death is inevitable.

When faced with the question, "What happens when you die?", people usually offer one of four answers:

1. You cease to exist
2. Your soul transfers to another body or form
3. You live a disembodied existence or
4. You live an embodied existence

Let's look at each of these in more detail. First, there is the idea that you cease to exist or are annihilated after death. Those who have a materialistic view of man or who do not believe in the existence of the soul will likely hold this view. For them, there is nothing after death. This life, from cradle to grave, is the totality of a person's existence. As one man put it, after death you just become worm food. As a result, there is no thought about life beyond the minutes and hours of the day. There is no accountability for any actions or concern for eternal consequences because there is nothing beyond the casket. "Now" is all we need to be concerned about because there is no "then."

For most people, the idea of no life after death is unsatisfying. Both now and throughout history, it seems the majority opinion has been that we do live in some way beyond the decay of our body. Some have thought the soul leaves the body at death and takes up residence in a place of departed spirits such as the Hebrews' Sheol or the Greeks' Hades. However, the soul is free to return, but not indwell the body. That's why provision was made to care for the soul on these return visits. Items such as food and drink were buried with the body so that the freed soul would not go hungry.

A second view which people have held is that the soul leaves the body and takes up residence in another body. This is called transmigration of the soul. With this view, there is accountability because the next assignment for your soul is determined by how you live now. One who is deemed a good soul in this life will inhabit a better body in the next. Conversely, a bad soul will move down the scale and inhabit an even less enjoyable body in the next. The interesting thing about this concept is that there is usually very little explanation about what the measuring stick is to determine good versus bad or who makes the judgment. It's just accepted that it happens. Many Eastern religions such as Hinduism teach this idea of transmigration, which is also called reincarnation. More recently, the actress Shirley McClain gained notoriety for claiming she had lived a number of past lives. Her books pushed the idea of transmigration to the forefront of popular culture.

A third idea that people offer to explain life after death is a disembodied existence. This answer usually corresponds with someone who views the human soul as simply part of the larger universal soul. Therefore, at death, the soul of the person returns to take its place as part of the cosmos. In contrast to annihilation and transmigration, which both eliminate the person, this view suggests the person goes on living, but with no bodily form. A good example is the Star Wars movie *The Empire Strikes Back*. Those who have seen the film will recall the last scene involves a party where the main characters, Luke Skywalker, Princess Leah, and Hans Solo are celebrating their victory at the Ewok camp. Also in attendance are the translucent, but recognizable, images of those who died, including Obi-Wan Kenobi and Darth Vader, sans the black mask and cape. The message of the scene is clear. People die, but they don't cease to exist. In fact, if their schedule allows, they're free to attend parties. In addition, this view of life after death is also one explanation why we have ghosts and other paranormal visitors.

A New Body

A fourth and final answer that is offered to the question of life after death is that the soul is immortal and will have a **new** embodied existence. This is the answer shaped by a Christian worldview. Paul explains this to the Corinthian church in chapter 15 of his first letter. Starting in verse 35, he tells them:

> [35] *But someone will ask, "How are the dead raised? With what kind of body do they come?"* [36] *Fool! What you sow does not come to life unless it dies.* [37] *And as for what you sow, you do not sow the body that is to be, but a bare seed, perhaps of wheat or of some other grain.* [38] *But God gives it a body as he has chosen, and to each kind of seed its own body.* [39] *Not all flesh is alike, but there is one flesh for human beings, another for animals, another for birds, and another for fish.* [40] *There are both heavenly bodies and earthly bodies, but the glory of the heavenly is one thing, and that of the earthly is another.* [41] *There is one glory of the sun, and another glory of the moon, and another glory of the stars; indeed, star differs from star in glory.*
> [42] *So it is with the resurrection of the dead. What is sown is perishable, what is raised is imperishable.* [43] *It is sown in dishonor, it is raised in glory. It is sown in weakness, it is raised in power.* [44] *It is sown a physical body, it is raised a spiritual body. If there is a physical body, there is also a spiritual body.* [45] *Thus it is written, "The first man, Adam, became a living being"; the last Adam became a life-giving spirit.* [46] *But it is not the spiritual that is first, but the physical, and then the spiritual.* [47] *The first man was from the earth, a man of dust; the second man is from heaven.* [48] *As was the man of dust, so are those who are of the dust; and as is the man of heaven, so are those who are of heaven.* [49] *Just as we have*

*borne the image of the man of dust, we will also bear the image of
the man of heaven.*

*⁵⁰ What I am saying, brothers and sisters, is this: flesh and blood
cannot inherit the kingdom of God, nor does the perishable inherit
the imperishable. ⁵¹ Listen, I will tell you a mystery! We will not all
die, but we will all be changed, ⁵² in a moment, in the twinkling
of an eye, at the last trumpet. For the trumpet will sound, and the
dead will be raised imperishable, and we will be changed. ⁵³ For
this perishable body must put on imperishability, and this mortal
body must put on immortality. ⁵⁴ When this perishable body puts
on imperishability, and this mortal body puts on immortality,
then the saying that is written will be fulfilled: "Death has been
swallowed up in victory." ⁵⁵ "Where, O death, is your victory?
Where, O death, is your sting?" ⁵⁶ The sting of death is sin, and
the power of sin is the law. ⁵⁷ But thanks be to God, who gives us
the victory through our Lord Jesus Christ.*

*⁵⁸ Therefore, my beloved, be steadfast, immovable, always
excelling in the work of the Lord, because you know that in the
Lord your labor is not in vain.⁷⁰*

Here Paul thoroughly and eloquently tells the church that those
who died in Christ can look forward to the resurrection of the dead.
Even more importantly, at the sound of the trumpet we will all be
changed and given a new body. Not a body that has been corrupted
by sin, but one which is "incorruptible and immortal." Death, man's
seemingly invincible foe, will be defeated once and for all. Man will
live on with a new body.

Furthermore, if you read the description of the new heaven and
earth and new Jerusalem given to us in Revelation, it's reasonable
to expect this embodied existence to be more, not less, than we
experience now. The idea of spending eternity sitting on a cloud
playing a harp is a quaint picture, but not a Biblical one.

This embodied existence generates other questions such as, what
will we do in heaven; will animals be present and a host of other

musings. Some answers we have now; for example, the Bible tells us we won't be married. Other answers we won't have until then. But we can be confident of this: because of Christ's resurrected body, we can look forward to ours.

The Message of the Stone

I walked one day
A long, long way
And came across an open space
The dead we buried in that place.

Before me was a granite stone,
Off by itself, it stood alone,
And on that stone there was a name,
Two dates, a dash, it was the same
As many other stones around
There alone upon a mound.
A date for birth, a date for death
The simple dash was only left.

A life, I thought, has now gone by,
The days I'm sure all seemed to fly,
And now a dash is left to say
This life has past, not one more day.

Some days seemed long, others short,
We bank them all, not one abort,
And then comes one, like all that past,
When God says now, this is your last.

And then alone, before God lay,
Not many words were had to say,
"Here is my life. The work I've done,
Here's all I did, this is the sum."

I wonder what did happen next,
As God stood there,
His gaze on him fixed?
What words were said
to Him who lay,

Life's challenges over,
the time has past
Our work is done but what will last?
Some are ashes, other gold,
Those done in faith will not grow old.

I thought while looking on that stone,
The name, the dates,
the dash that shown,
What impact will my work, the sum,
Will eternity be richer
when my life is done?

Jerry Twombley[71]

DISCUSSION QUESTIONS

1) In your own words, give a description of the soul.

2) Excluding special revelation, what indicators could you use that point to the immortality of the soul?

3) What are the four primary answers thinkers have given to the question, "What happens to you after you die?"

4) What are the present personal ramifications of each view?

5) Can you name any books or movies that suggest an answer to the question of immortality?

6) What view do you think most people hold today and why?

7) What kind of questions can you ask in conversation to stimulate a person's thinking in this area?

7

---------·•·---------

GOOD AND EVIL

Good and evil both increase at compound interest. That is why little decisions you and I make every day are of such infinite importance.

C. S. Lewis
Mere Christianity[72]

If you were to survey many of our most memorable fables and stories, you would find a number of them contain a common theme. Forces of good and evil locked in conflict with one another for control. But what is good and what is evil? Are they unchanging, objective measures that were established before the beginning of time and will stand forever? Or are they relative, dictated by circumstances or determined by the individual? Or is it possible that there is no such thing as good or evil? The "g" word and the "e" word are just subjective descriptions of particular actions or circumstances.

To answer these questions, it is first necessary to arrive at some agreement about the existence and nature of good and evil. This is an issue that has challenged philosophers throughout the ages. For Christians thinkers, this topic has been particularly important because inevitably Christians seem to wrestle with the question, "If God is good, why is there so much evil in the world?" Another way to say it is: If God is good, why do death, disease, war, famine and a myriad of other atrocities fill the evening news?

Answers from History

Every civilization sought to give some explanation as to "why bad things happen?" The early Greeks paid particular attention to this matter. Heraclitus, who hailed from Ephesus and lived around 500 B.C., taught that good and evil were actually opposites that co-exist. In his view, a combination of opposites in the universe creates harmony like low and high notes combine to create musical harmony. God sees the harmony. Man just sees the opposites.

However, according to Heraclitus, as man uses reason, he can understand the universal laws that govern our existence and live in harmony with them. Doing so then allows man to avoid evil and live what is considered a good life.

Protagoras, who lived in Athens about the same time as Heraclitus, did not see good and evil in the same way. Recall that he was the man who saw "man as the measure of all things." By that, he did not mean "man" as a community, but "man" as the individual. Therefore, Protagoras taught that each man was left to decide for himself what was good and evil. As a result, morality was not something determined by laws that applied to all men, but rather it was up to each person to establish his own code by which to live. It's an interesting idea, and actually an appealing one, because it caters to our natural self-centeredness. Practically though, it did not gain much support.

In fact, Socrates who lived from 469 to 399 BC disagreed with the idea that good and evil were personally determined. It was Socrates' firm belief that there must be a basic principle of right and wrong, a measure which would apply far beyond the beliefs of any one individual.[73] Consequently, Socrates continually wrestled with the questions, "What is good?" and "What is the highest good?" by which all things in the universe should be judged. His conclusion was that knowledge is the highest good. In his view, if goodness exists, it can be known. So a person should pursue knowing goodness because once it is known, he can choose the good. In Socrates' view, men only act "bad," because they don't have knowledge of what is good.

Plato, who was a student of Socrates, took these ideas one step further and saw the problem of good and evil related to the nature of the universe. Recall that Plato taught the universe is two stories, upper and lower. The upper story contains ideals, and the lower story, matter. The lower story is fleeting and changing and a mere representation of the ideals resident in the upper story. To understand the lower story, we use our senses. To understand the upper story, we use reason. That's why for Plato the highest good is a life of reason. It also explains why he saw the lower story as evil and the upper story as good.

Plato's disciple, Aristotle, took these ideas another step. Though he disagreed with Plato on the nature of the upper and lower stories, he did concur that "the full realization of a life of reason was the highest good for man."[74]

However, amidst the voices of these philosophical giants, there were dissenting opinions. Epicurus, who was mentioned in previous chapters, saw pleasure as man's main pursuit and highest good. According to him, pain and unfulfilled desire are evil. The Stoics, who were also influential about the same time, espoused similar ideas. They saw man's highest good as living in harmony with the universe. Evil wasn't real for them. It was simply the result of living in disharmony with the rule and laws of the universe, which they believed could be understood by reason.

These ideas stood for nearly 800 years in the West until Christian thinkers such as Augustine offered another explanation for evil that the Greeks had not presented. Augustine thought the problem of evil was especially challenging because Christians believed that God is good and all He created is good. So how can evil exist in a good world created by a good God? The answer is simple. Evil is not an essence or substance in itself, but rather the privation of good. In other words, evil is a lack of good in things, not a thing in itself. Evil then is like rust on a car or rot on a tree. Neither of those is a substance in itself and could not exist if the "good" (in this case a car and tree) did not exist.

A few centuries later, another key Christian thinker, Thomas Aquinas, more fully developed this explanation of evil. We will examine his ideas a little later in this chapter, but first we want to consider other key thoughts that philosophers after Augustine offered to explain good and evil.

For the most part, their explanations are a derivation of ideas that we've already explored. For example, Thomas Hobbes, who lived in the sixteenth century, saw good and evil as relative. Much like the Epicureans, he saw pleasure as good and pain as evil. However, he also recognized what may be pleasurable for one man is painful to another. Or what may be pleasurable at one point in time may be painful at another. Therefore, he concluded you could not say anything was absolutely good or evil. It depended on the person and circumstance.

Other influential thinkers such as John Locke promoted similar views. In fact, Locke, who lived from 1632 to 1704, taught that we learn what is good and bad from experience. Locke "made morality largely a matter of enlightened self-interest: that is, one is good because being good pays the highest dividends in individual pleasure."[75]

Following these men, a number of thinkers suggested that the goodness of an action is determined by more than just what it does for the individual. Philosophers began to advocate that for an act to be good, it must also benefit society. Men like John Stuart Mill, who lived in the 1800s said that the measure of good was, "the greatest good for the greatest number." So in other words, good and evil were not determined by universal divine laws, but by social relationships.

Building on the ideas of Mills, influential philosophers in the 1900s such as William James and John Dewey, insisted that "the human individual, as a social unit, is the ultimate measure of good and evil."[76] They were quite emphatic in teaching that good is what serves the group and the individual in the group. So the nature of good and evil was determined in social settings rather than by a universal principle. Furthermore, it was difficult to declare anything as absolutely good or evil because you could only tell in the context of a group. So clearly good and evil were relative.

These ideas of Mills, James, Dewey and others who followed them are not surprising if you remember the shift in thinking that took place from the Renaissance through the time of the Enlightenment. For the most part, post-Enlightenment thinkers rejected the idea of knowing the upper story using reason. Later, many actually doubted or even denied the existence of an upper story. For them, good and evil had to be determined by man, because you could not say with surety that God or universals existed. S. E. Frost summarizes their thinking in this way.

> In this modern treatment of the subject, good and bad are not written in the nature of the universe, but are determined by social factors. The emphasis is placed upon the consequences of one's act in the experiences of others. The idea of a God setting down absolutely defined moral laws is gone. Also the idea that an evil act angers God while a good act makes Him happy is missing. Here is a relative morality, and the determiner of good and bad is the effect

of the act upon the lives of other human individuals now living or to live in the future.[77]

Answers for Our Time

We've considered what thinkers throughout history have concluded, but what do people in our day think about the existence and nature of good and evil? Is it something inherent in the universe to be discovered in time by all who seek to know it? Or are good and evil relative to the person and setting and not fixed by some common measuring stick? As we have seen throughout history, there never seems to be one explanation that satisfies everybody at any one time. In our day, it is no different. Typically, one of these four answers is given to the question, "What is good and evil?"

1. Good and evil are relative and don't exist.
2. Good and evil are independent, equally powerful forces set in conflict.
3. Evil is created and it exists as an essence or antithesis of good.
4. Evil is not created, but is actually the privation of good.

Good and Evil are Relative

Let's consider each of these options. First, good and evil are relative and don't exist. Prior to 9/11, this was probably the most common answer of modern man. To say otherwise was to admit that there are universals which govern all people in all circumstances. As I suggested earlier, post-Enlightenment thinkers have largely rejected this idea. Furthermore, even though relativism has always been an option, it really ascended to prominence as humanism began to dominate man's thinking. In fact, relativism seems to be a natural outcome of putting man on the throne as his own judge. There is no accountability to any higher power. Man is the highest power and sets his own standard. Therefore, he looks only to himself to determine whether an action is good or bad.

The obvious flaw in this argument is that a relative view of good and evil creates the potential for freedom to run amok and for justice to be fickle. Without a fixed standard by which to make judgments, liberty is without bounds and justice is nearly impossible to administer. That creates major problems because for any society to function well, both liberty and justice must exist in proper relationship to one another. If they do not, abuse of personal freedoms and ludicrous judgments often occur. In fact, they are almost inevitable when man, and not God or universals, are the source for final answers.

Good and Evil Are Independent Forces

Today, there are many who still believe that good and evil exist. One way to explain their existence is that good and evil are independent, equally powerful forces set in conflict with one another. The *Star Wars* movies are a good example of how this idea is expressed in our culture. Remember, a key theme of the story is the struggle between the Force, which is good, and the Dark Side, which is evil. Each competes to win the affections and allegiance of the characters. No explanation is given for the origin of the Force or the reason it exists. We are just supposed to accept that the Force is real and beckons for control.

For those who accept that there is evil in the universe, this is a simple, but ineffective explanation. The problem with this answer is there is usually no account for how good and evil came to be or why they are in conflict. In addition, we are always unsure which will win, though historically, the moral of most stories has been that good triumphs over evil.

Good and Evil Are Created Entities

A third answer that is sometimes given to explain the existence of good and evil is that evil is created and it exists as an essence or the antithesis of good. Early Greeks suggested good and evil created a harmony in the universe in the same way low and high notes create harmony in a musical composition. Others have tried to say that God created evil. Their reasoning is as follows:

1. God is the creator of everything.
2. Evil is something.
3. Therefore, God is the author of evil.

If you accept all three of these statements as true, the logical conclusion is that God is the creator of evil. However, if you believe God is good, this cannot be true, because then He would be the cause of evil. That is contrary to His nature or essence. So then what do you do with these statements? Augustine and especially Aquinas were helpful in actually formulating the fourth explanation of evil. For them, evil is a privation of good.

Evil Is a Privation of Good

The key is not to reject the three statements, but reject the premise of statement two, that evil is something. Evil is not a something, but is rather a privation of a good thing that God has made. Privation is probably a word that most of us don't use frequently, but it is very important that we understand what it means. Privation is not the same as absence. Norm Geisler provides a helpful explanation of the two words in his book on Thomas Aquinas. Geisler states:

> *Aquinas is quick to note that privation is not the same as absence. Sight is absent in a stone as well as a blind person. But absence in a stone is not privation. Privation is the lack of something that ought to be there. Since the stone by nature ought not to see, it is not deprived of sight as is a blind person. Evil then is the deprivation of some good that ought to be there.*[78]

In other words, evil is not an actual entity, but the corruption of an entity. ***Evil only exists as a corruption.*** Therefore, if there is nothing good to corrupt, evil could not exist. However, to say that evil is not an entity, is not to suggest that evil is not real. Physical privations, such as blindness, and moral privations such as starving a person to death, are very real. Their impact is real and the pain and frustration they cause are real.

What About Good?

Of the four explanations for evil that we've considered, the idea of privation is the one that best fits a Christian worldview. However, if we are to agree with this definition, we must also have a clear idea of what is "good." As we have already discovered, defining what is good has created debate over the centuries. For the Christian, goodness is not relative or illusory. It is real because it exists in the character and nature of God. Therefore, to judge the "goodness" of any thing or circumstance, we look to God's character and nature as a reference point. To state it another way, something is good when it's in harmony or agreement with God's design, purpose, and order for that thing. The meanings of each of these words in this context are important. When we speak of design, we mean that nothing exists by chance, but God had an idea in mind when He created all things. When we speak of purpose, we mean that all things were created for a reason. Again, nothing exists by chance or accident. Finally, when we speak of order, we mean that everything is created to be in a particular and proper relationship with all other created things. So when God looked at all He created and declared it good, it was in harmony and agreement with His design, purpose, and order.

For the Christian, this idea of good is extremely important for three reasons. First, it gives us an understanding of what a "good" life is compared to what others have suggested. A Christian's measure of a good life is not **just** pleasure as the Epicureans propose or what **only** benefits society as the Pragmatists say, but rather it is choosing what's in harmony with God's design, purpose and order. The implications of this idea are significant and greater than we have time and space to address in this chapter because they profoundly shape how you live your life. In addition, it brings to light a critical reason why we need to know God. He is the only One who is good. Therefore, if we are to have a right view of good, we must have a right view of God.

A second reason why it's vital to have a right definition of good is it clarifies our understanding of evil. Recall that we said evil is a privation of good. Therefore, if we are unclear as to what is good, we will be unsure of what is evil. In other words, knowledge of good equips us to recognize evil in politics, business, relationships, and in every sphere of life.

Finally, it is important that we have a clear view of good because we have a responsibility to infuse culture with goodness. In doing so, we reflect God's character and we prevent evil from taking root and spreading. As Edmund Burke stated so precisely, "All that is necessary for the triumph of evil is for good men to do nothing."

Do not be overcome with evil, but overcome evil with good.

Romans 12:21[79]

Discussion Questions

1) What are the four primary answers thinkers have given to explain the existence of good and evil?

2) How does a Christian explain the origin and existence of evil?

3) How would you explain the nature of good?

4) How do most people around you explain the problem of evil in the world?

5) How does popular culture, i.e., movies, books, TV, attempt to explain the nature of good and evil?

6) How does the Holocaust fit into a Christian understanding of good and evil?

7) How has evil impacted your life and how have you responded to it?

8

---·•·---

THEOLOGY—WHAT ABOUT GOD?

To most people God is an inference, not a reality. He is a deduction from evidence which they consider adequate, but He remains personally unknown to the individual.

A. W. Tozer
The Pursuit of God. The 30 Day Experience [80]

So far we have examined the issues that shape worldview as individual elements, but we must not forget that a person's worldview is formed at the convergence of three major presuppositions of thought about God, man, and existence (Figure 11b). Each component influences the others so it is difficult to say that any one issue is more important than another. However, if there is one that might be most significant, it would probably be what a person thinks about God. That's because, although most people agree the bottom two circles exist and relate in some way, many doubt or even deny the existence and relationship of the top circle to the bottom two. So what do people think about God? That's a big question to answer in just a few short paragraphs when millions and millions of pages have been written addressing the matter. However, as A. W. Tozer points out in *Knowledge of the Holy*, what we think about God may be the most significant idea we hold.

How Worldview Is Formed

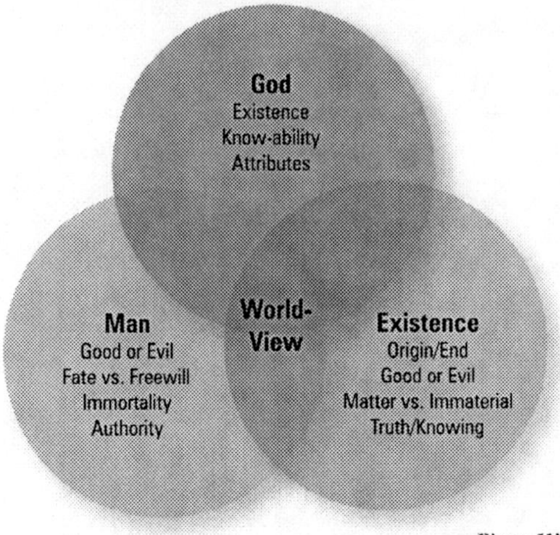

Figure 11b

What comes into our minds when we think about God is the most important thing about us. The history of mankind will probably show that no people has ever risen above its religion, and man's spiritual history will positively demonstrate that no religion has ever been greater than its idea of God. Worship is pure or base as the worshiper entertains high or low thoughts of God.

For this reason the gravest question before the Church is always God Himself, and the most portentous fact about any man is not what he at a given time may say or do, but what he in his deep heart conceives God to be like. [81]

What then do people in our day think about when they contemplate God? I would like to suggest there are six major ideas that people believe or hold to with respect to God, His attributes, and His relationship to man.

What Do People Think about God?

For many in our day, God could be described as **polytheistic, pantheistic or monotheistic.** These are views that were likely dominant prior to the Enlightenment. Since then, three other ideas about God have gained prominence in the West. Those views are **deism, agnosticism and atheism.** Let's take a moment to look at each of these.

Polytheism—Not One, But Many Gods

Polytheistic

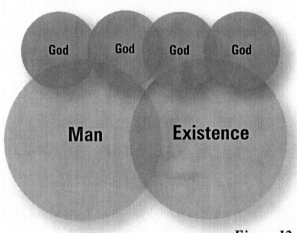

Figure 12

Polytheism is the idea that God is actually many gods and is illustrated using the circles diagram (Figure 12). Greek and Roman mythologies are examples of polytheism. According to those systems of belief, there are gods who have certain domains or responsibilities. For example, the Roman god Neptune is god of the sea, which defines the limits of his domain and locus of his power. However, not every god is male. Nor does every god have a particular geographic domain. For example, the Roman goddess Venus is the goddess of love. So her sphere of influence is not bound by space, but rather by a particular affair or concern of man. In this case, the affairs of the heart, which are related to love. No one god has all the power, but they all interact with humans in various ways bringing about good or bad depending on the circumstances. In fact, in many cases the gods themselves are flawed. They bicker and connive out of self-interest or misdirected passion. In many ways, they're given to the same problems as humans, though they possess powers greater than mankind. Presently, Hinduism is an example of polytheism.

In addition, there is a variation of polytheism called **henotheism**. Henotheism is the idea that there are many gods, but their domains are limited to a particular geographic area or land. An example of henotheism is given to us in the II Kings, chapter 17.

> *Then the king of Assyria brought people from Babylon, Cuthah, Ava, Hamath, and from Sepharvaim, and placed them in the cities of Samaria instead of the children of Israel; and they took possession of Samaria and dwelt in its cities. And it was so, at the beginning of their dwelling there, that they did not fear the Lord; therefore the Lord sent lions among them, which killed some of them. So they spoke to the king of Assyria, saying, "The nations whom you have removed and placed in the cities of Samaria do not know the rituals of the God of the land; therefore He has sent lions among them, and indeed, they are killing them because they do not know the rituals of the God of the land." Then the king of Assyria commanded, saying, "Send there one of the priests whom you brought from there; let him go and dwell there, and let him teach them the rituals of the God of the land."[82]*

The nation Israel has been carried off in captivity and the king of Assyria sent in his people to possess the land. They encounter trouble and believe it is because they do not know how to appease the gods who dwell there. As a result, the king sends Hebrew priests back to Samaria to teach them "the rituals of the God of the land." The Jews who were sent back then took Babylonian occupants as wives and had children with them. That's why Samaritans are seen as half breeds and squatters on a land promised to Israel and despised by the Jews of Jesus' day (John 4). However, what's most interesting is this came about because the Assyrian king held a henotheistic view of God. That was the reason he sent Hebrew priests back into the land.

Pantheism—All Parts of Existence Combine to Make God

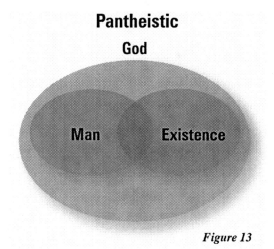

Figure 13

A second major belief about God is **pantheism.** This is the idea that the universe taken or conceived of as a whole, is God. So God is not an independent being. Rather the combined materials and forces that make up the world constitute God. Figure 13 illustrates how this might be expressed using the three circles. In this view, God's nature is diminished while material nature is elevated, for we and everything around us possess some degree of "godness." This view also suggests that God is not immutable or unchanging, for as matter decays, so does God. In fact, carried to the extreme, this position implies that if the world did not exist, God would not exist, which is not a real confidence builder in times of trouble. Though many ancient tribal religions are pantheistic, we still find this idea alive and well in many New Age religion and philosophies.

Monotheism—One God, Not Many

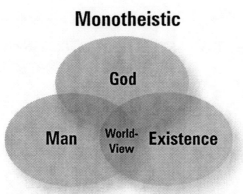

Monotheistic

Figure 14

In contrast to the two views we've considered so far, **monotheism** is a view that God is neither multiple deities nor distributed throughout the material world. Rather God is distinct, separate, and most importantly, a single entity. Figure 14 illustrates how a monotheistic view of God looks using the three circles. Jews and Christians understand God in this way primarily because this is how He has revealed Himself. For example, in Deuteronomy 6:4, God declares, *"Hear O Israel, The Lord our God is one."* This "oneness" is significant because it establishes a clear authority in the universe, across time, and ultimately in the life of the individual. Furthermore, in contrast to a deistic view, which we will discuss in the next paragraph, this view of God shows Him to be engaged with His creation. For the Christian, the Incarnation and the Word becoming flesh (John 1:14) give evidence of this fact.

Deism—God Is There, but Leaves Things Alone

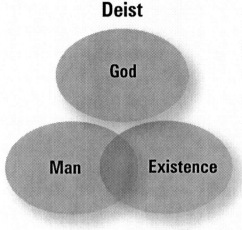

Figure 15

A fourth view of God, which developed primarily after the Enlightenment, is **deism**. This is the idea that God exists, but has intentionally separated Himself from creation. In other words, He was involved in creation and establishing the principles that govern existence but has voluntarily removed himself from existence and the lower story. Figure 15 shows how the three circles can be used to illustrate this concept. Deists often compare God to a watchmaker, who designed the watch, built it, wound it, set it in motion, and then let it run without intervention. The difference between deism and monotheism is significant. Although each view believes in God, what they believe about God is very different. With deism the supernatural or spiritual does not interface with the natural or material. Another way to say it is—the upper story and lower story exist but do not interact in any way. For example, according to deists, Jesus Christ was super human, but not divine. In fact, Thomas Jefferson, who was a deist, created his own version of the Bible, called the Jefferson Bible, which eliminates any reference to Jesus being God, as well as any reference to miracles. For the deist, the supernatural may exist, but it never enters our world. We are on our own.

One other point worth noting is that philosophers refer to deism as a closed system, where as every other view we have considered so far is an open system. In other words, there is a natural, material world, but it is "open" to interaction from the supernatural world. Deism denies that possibility.

Agnosticism—God May Exist, but We Can't Know For Sure

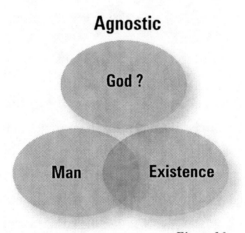

Figure 16

Another view that developed post-Enlightenment is the idea that God may or may not exist. We just can't know for sure. This idea is called **agnosticism**. Agnosticism is a word composed of two Greek words that help us remember what it means. The first word is the Greek word "gnosis" which means to know. The second word is the negative prefix, "a" which means not. It is similar to the English prefix "un." So in this case, agnostic literally means "not know." Figure 16 shows how you might use the three circles to illustrate this view. Compared to deism, which accepts that God exists, agnosticism holds that we cannot say for certain that He does; and if He does, we can't say for sure we know what He is like. That's why there is a question mark in the top circle.

This view of God has probably always existed in some form as mankind has struggled to understand the world around him and answer life's big questions. However, an argument could be made that this view gained significant prominence as a result of the post-Enlightenment perspective of truth and knowing. Recall that men such as Kant promoted the idea that reason is the only trusted way we can know the world, and reason cannot be used to know the upper story. Since God dwells in the upper story, we can't use reason to know Him. Therefore, we can't say anything sure about Him. That is agnosticism in a nutshell.

Atheism—There Is No God

While agnostics say we can't know for sure if God exists, atheists are certain: there is no God. Like agnosticism, the word atheism is made up of two Greek words that can help us remember its meaning. The first word is the Greek word "theos," which is the word for "God." The second word is the negative prefix "a" which means "no or not." Therefore, the word atheism, literally means "not or no God."

Figure 17 shows how atheism could be explained using the three circles. Notice how in contrast to every other view of God, there is no top circle in this illustration. Throughout history, there have been people who explained God this way. It is likely that the development of a scientific, materialistic view of life contributed to the wider acceptance of this idea.

Atheist

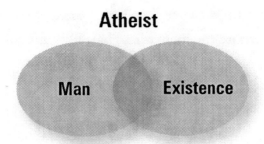

Figure 17

For scholars, these explanations may be an oversimplification, but it seems as man began to grow in his knowledge of the seen and unseen material world, and as technological advances allowed him to control parts of his environment in unprecedented ways, the idea of God became outdated and useless. Man began to believe all that needed to be known could eventually be discovered and explained through scientific inquiry. God and faith were only needed to explain the world where science couldn't provide answers. A person educated and trained in the sciences would not need such ideas, because eventually, through biology, chemistry, and physics all the answers we need and that exist can be and will be found. What about religion? It is for the immature, uneducated, and unsophisticated. In short, in his knowledge, man became haughty.

Why Does Our View of God Matter?

Modern man has given considerable time to the problem of whether or not God exists, but an equally important question to consider is "Why is it so crucial to have a defined view of God?" Many would conclude that answering this question is useful for the "professional" theologian or pastor but has little practical value in everyday life. Theology, for most people, is one of those subjects best left to the "experts." Yet each one of us is a theologian in that we hold some view of God, whether it is well thought out or not. More importantly, our "theology" has highly critical and practical ramifications. First, a wrong view of God is the fertile soil from which idolatry springs. Tozer, commenting on this fact, observes:

> *Among the sins to which the human heart is prone, hardly any other more hateful to God than idolatry, for idolatry is at bottom a libel on His character. The idolatrous heart assumes that God is other than He is—in itself a monstrous sin—and substitutes for the true God one made after its own likeness.*[83]

He then adds later in the same chapter:

> *Let us beware lest we in our pride accept an erroneous notion that idolatry consists only in kneeling before visible objects of adoration, and that civilized peoples are therefore free from it. The essence of idolatry is the entertainment of thoughts about God that are unworthy of Him. It begins in the mind and may be present where no overt act of worship has taken place.*[84]

I find Tozer's observations helpful because we often don't think of idolatry as something with which we struggle. Idol worship is a challenge for uncivilized savages, not for us. Yet, no matter how "religious" we are, a wrong view of God will lead to the very thing that God forbids in the second commandment.

A second problem that comes from a wrong view of God is heresy. Tozer contends that "there is scarcely an error in doctrine or a failure in applying Christian ethics that cannot be traced finally to imperfect and ignoble thoughts about God."[85] History bears this out. The nation Israel's sin in the desert at Mount Sinai (Exodus 32) when they worshiped the golden calf was not just worshiping a false God but rather worshiping a wrong view of the true God. They said the calf was the god that "led them from Egypt." It was clearly idolatry, but it was born out of heresy. This is just one example. In the early church, men such as Marcion, Manichee and Arius all taught ideas that were ultimately declared heretical by the Church. They all began from a wrong view of God.

A third reason why having a right view of God is important is because it determines how we respond when faced with a problem or crisis. We had one example earlier in this chapter in II Kings 17. Recall the Babylonian king sent the Hebrew priest back into Samaria to deal with "the gods of the land." Another helpful example is Rahab the harlot. Rahab's story is given to us in chapter two of the book of Joshua.

> *Then Joshua son of Nun sent two men secretly from Shittim as spies, saying, "Go, view the land, especially Jericho." So they went, and entered the house of a prostitute whose name was Rahab, and spent the night there. [2] The king of Jericho was told, "Some Israelites have come here tonight to search out the land." [3] Then the king of Jericho sent orders to Rahab, "Bring out the men who have come to you, who entered your house, for they have come only to search out the whole land." [4] But the woman took the two men and hid them. Then she said, "True, the men came to me, but I did not know where they came from. [5] And when it was time to close the gate at dark, the men went out. Where the men went I do not know. Pursue them quickly, for you can overtake them." [6] She had, however, brought them up to the roof and hidden them with the stalks of flax that she had laid out on the roof. [7] So the men pursued them on the way to the Jordan as far as the fords. As soon as the pursuers had gone out, the gate was shut. [8] Before they went to sleep, she came up to them on the roof [9] and said to the men: "I know that the Lord has given you the land, and that dread of you has fallen on us, and that all the inhabitants of the land melt in fear before you. [10] For we have heard how the Lord dried up the water of the Red Sea before you when you came out of Egypt, and what you did to the two kings of the Amorites that were beyond the*

Jordan, to Sihon and Og, whom you utterly destroyed. [11] As soon as we heard it, our hearts melted, and there was no courage left in any of us because of you. The Lord your God is indeed God in heaven above and on earth below. [12] Now then, since I have dealt kindly with you, swear to me by the Lord that you in turn will deal kindly with my family. Give me a sign of good faith [13] that you will spare my father and mother, my brothers and sisters, and all who belong to them, and deliver our lives from death." [14] The men said to her, "Our life for yours! If you do not tell this business of ours, then we will deal kindly and faithfully with you when the Lord gives us the land."[86]

Here Rahab is faced with a real problem. Foreigners have invaded her home. What should she do? Sound the alarm? Turn them in? Abandon her house? Run for her life? Those are all options worth considering. But she didn't choose any of them. Instead, she hides the spies and protects them. Why? The answer lies in her theology, in her view of God. She states it starting in verse 9 and sums it up for us with her declaration in verse 11, "*The Lord your God is indeed God in heaven above and on earth below.*" Rahab believed something about God that caused her to radically change the course of her life and the life of her family. If you were to follow her story to the first chapter of Matthew, you will discover Rahab is actually part of the lineage of the Lord Jesus Christ. That's amazing, but I would suggest she would never have made the decision to hide the spies if she had not viewed God the way she did. Her theology had profound ramifications in her life. And so does yours.

How Can We Know God?

If you accept what was just stated as true, then the next key question is, "How can we know God?" How can we know which of the ideas that we've discussed so far is correct? For the Christian the answer to that question is tied to our view of truth and knowing. Once again this illustrates how these issues are interrelated. In the first chapter, we established that we come to know cognitively, empirically, and by revelation. All of them are important, but without

General Revelation	Special Revelation
Nature, Man, and History	The Bible and Jesus Christ

revelation we could not come to understand and know God. Let me explain. Let's say I wanted to get to know Peyton Manning, the great quarterback of the Indianapolis Colts. I could go to his house. I could pound on his door. I could shout at him, but for me to get to know him, two things would have to happen. First, he must make a move toward me. Second, he is going to have to "reveal" something about himself. I may observe it or he may tell it to me directly. For me to know him, he must provide some revelation of himself. The same is true of God. For me to know God, He must make a move toward me and reveal something of Himself. The beauty of this story is that He has.

God's revelation of Himself falls into two categories for most theologians: general revelation and special revelation. **General revelation** includes the created world, the nature of man and history. It is by these we can learn about God. For example, in Psalm 19, the psalmist exclaims, "The heavens declare the glory of the Lord," and in Genesis 1:26 we read, "Let Us make man in Our image."[87] But these are not enough to lead us to salvation because **special** or **specific revelation** is required. That comes through the Bible and the person of Jesus Christ. Another way to think of it is the

Written Word and the Living Word. It is through these we come to understand God's plan of salvation.

Many people in our day will struggle with these categories. Primarily because the post-Enlightenment mind holds that we cannot know God with certainty at all. These categories of general and special revelation are not relevant because many doubt we can know anything about God. Furthermore, the strong cultural value of tolerance makes it difficult to reach agreement that there is One True God who has revealed Himself in such a way that we can know Him. For the Christian, we believe that God has made Himself known though not completely, and that there will come a time in the future when Christ Himself will be revealed as He is. Paul reminds us in I Corinthians, "For now we see in a mirror, dimly, but then we will see face to face. Now I know only in part; then I will know fully, even as I have been fully known."[88]

> *The heavens are telling the glory of God; and the firmament proclaims his handiwork. Day to day pours forth speech, and night to night declares knowledge.*
>
>   *Psalm 19:1-3*[89]

DISCUSSION QUESTIONS

1) Without looking at your notes, draw the six different views of God using the three circles to illustrate each idea.

2) Besides the examples given in the reading, can you think of ways or places where these views of God are expressed in culture today?

3) Which view of God do you believe most people hold today and why?

4) According to the reading there are three reasons why is it important to have a right view of God. What are they?

5) Can you think of any other reasons why having a right view of God might be critical?

6) As you reflect on your own life, how has your view of God changed over the years and why?

9

———— ❖ ————

IMPLICATIONS FOR
CULTURAL ENGAGEMENT AND EVANGELISM

*The object of opening the mind, as of opening the mouth, is to
shut it again on something solid.*

G. K. Chesterton
Autobiography[90]

In the first chapter, we stated that one of the goals of our study is to equip us to communicate the reality of a Christian worldview at every point of culture we touch. To simply gain knowledge, but not use it to speak truth and demonstrate love to the people around us, has the potential of creating an intellectual gated community. In this "community," we work to create a pleasant life for ourselves, while ignoring or criticizing the decay around us. We gain knowledge, but we don't use that learning to transform culture or reach people with the gospel. Clearly, this way of thinking is counter to the Great Commission, which instructs us to go into the world. However, as the world in which we live moves more and more to a secular consensus, it creates a number of challenges for Christians today. Two results of those challenges are a lack of cultural engagement on our part and ineffective evangelism methods. Each is worth considering in more detail.

A Lack of Cultural Engagement

By "lack of cultural engagement" I mean the church has removed itself from the places of influence that shape the world in which we all live. Media, art, government, and education are all areas that have been dominated by a secular point of view. Why? In my opinion, for the past 150 years, the church has taken the salvational mandate given to us in Matthew 28:18-20 more seriously than the creational mandate given to us in Genesis 1. In Matthew, we are commanded to go and make disciples, but in Genesis we are first told to rule and have dominion over all the earth. To only see the gospel as an evangelistic tool is to limit the full impact of the Good News. The intent of the gospel is not just to redeem individual souls but also to reorder culture. Ken Myers addresses this issue more fully in the following excerpt from a letter he wrote to Mars Hill Audio subscribers:

> *There are many Christian pundits and ministries dedicated to understanding contemporary culture solely for the sake of becoming better evangelists. But I believe that Christians make a great mistake if they separate proclamation, that is, announcing of the basic truths of the gospel, from faithfulness, that is, living out of all of the consequences of the gospel.*
>
> *It is possible to reduce the Gospel to a form of therapy. That is, it is possible to assume that the basic questions of life are well-asked and well-answered by the world and then order our careers, our relationships, our engagement with creation, even our prayers in accordance with a worldly worldview. It is possible to assume that our culture's basic understanding of reality is essentially sound, that its institutions are essentially good and just and fitting, in need of only minor adjustment and a religious appendix, and then order our lives in accordance with our culture's assumptions about things....*
>
> *It is possible to do that, but it is not the message of the Bible. I'm not saying that the gospel is not a message of hope, nor am I*

suggesting that it's improper to look to Christ for comfort. What I am saying is that we are not faithful disciples if we assume that we can order our lives any way we want to, knowing that Jesus will be there to encourage and lift us up when we feel down. Jesus is not there just to help us with our projects; He is the one who tells us what projects we should be pursuing.[91]

Another contributing factor to our lack of cultural engagement is that the church and most Christians have been more upper story focused than balanced in their view of the world. (See Chapter 2 for discussion on upper and lower story.) As a result, over the past century and a half, the church has placed greater importance on the spiritual and heavenly things of life than temporal and earthly things. This way of thinking has created a problem that many have labeled "the sacred/secular dilemma." This dilemma is created because we often compartmentalize our lives into sacred areas and secular areas. We think activities that are spiritual, such as church attendance and prayer, are "sacred" and somehow more pleasing to God. The mundane, profane activities, such as work and eating are secular, and therefore unimportant. Sound familiar? It should because that is how many committed faithful evangelical Christians live. However, this view of life it is not what God intended. A. W. Tozer in his book *The Pursuit of God* dedicates a whole chapter to this issue titled, "The Sacrament of Living." Tozer's insights can help resolve this dilemma. He writes:

We tend to divide our total life into two departments. We come unconsciously to recognize two sets of actions. The first are performed with a feeling of satisfaction and a firm assurance that they are pleasing to God. These are the sacred acts and they are usually thought to be prayer, Bible reading, hymn singing, church attendance and such other acts as spring directly from faith. They may be known by the fact that they would have no direct relation to this world, and would have no meaning whatsoever except as faith shows us another world, "a house not made with hands, eternal in the heavens" (II Corinthians 5:1).

Over against these sacred acts are the secular ones. They include all of the ordinary activities of life which we share with the sons and daughters of Adam: eating, sleeping, working, looking after the needs of the body and performing our dull and prosaic duties here on earth. These we often do reluctantly and with many misgivings, often apologizing to God for what we consider a waste of time and strength. The upshot of this is that we are uneasy most of the time. We go about our common tasks with a feeling of deep frustration, telling ourselves pensively that there is a better day coming when we shall slough off this earthly shell and be bothered no more with the affairs of this world.

This is the old sacred-secular antithesis. Most Christians are caught in its trap. They cannot get a satisfactory adjustment between the claims of the two worlds. They try to walk the tightrope between two kingdoms and they find no peace in either.

I believe this state of affairs to be wholly unnecessary. We have gotten ourselves on the horns of a dilemma, true enough, but the dilemma is not real. It is a creature of misunderstanding. The sacred-secular antithesis has no foundation in the New Testament.[92]

If you accept what I have just suggested as true, the key question then is what can we do about it? First, take the creational mandate as seriously as the salvational mandate. Live in response to our Savior, but also in response to our Creator. Demonstrate by your actions that all of life is sacred and all of life deserves our attention. Start with the places where you impact culture now. Be a just employer. Be hospitable in your neighborhood. Order your time as though you know there is a Sabbath. Sharing the reality of Christ in your life doesn't always require words. By the way you live you give evidence of a different understanding of how things really are.

Whatever you do, do as though working for God, not for men.

So that your daily life will win the respect of outsiders

Also, take opportunity to communicate the truth of the gospel into every area of life you touch even if you never use a Bible verse. In his essay "Christian Apologetics" in the volume *God in the Dock,* C. S. Lewis challenges us in this area:

> *We can make people attend to the Christian point of view for half and hour or so; but the moment they have gone away from our lecture or laid down our article, they are plunged back into a world where the opposite position is taken for granted. As long as that situation exists, widespread success is simply impossible. We must attack the enemy's lines of communication. What we want is not more little books about Christianity, but more little books by Christians on other subjects—with their Christianity latent.*[93]

If Lewis is correct, and I believe he is, it is important that we have Christians trained for every field of endeavor so that a Christian worldview can be brought to bear in every area of life. However, even for those who are passionate about sharing their faith, evangelism in the West can be difficult today—not because the gospel is less relevant, but often because our approach is.

As we have read in previous chapters, there have been some seismic shifts in thinking throughout the past decades that greatly impact how the gospel is received today. We can point to many factors, but in my opinion, the most important development is that the presuppositions upon which the Christian faith is built are no longer widely accepted.

Those presuppositions include:

1. The existence of universals or absolutes;
2. A thesis/antithesis understanding of truth; and
3. A material and immaterial view of the world.

Let's consider each of these. Foundational to a Christian worldview is the conviction that there are universals or absolutes—truths that are handed down and apply to all men at all times. For Christians, these universals or absolutes are laws that a personal God has set in place to govern life. They are unchangeable and applicable in all scenarios and exist outside of any personal choice. They are not to be defined by the individual, but are designed into the nature of things.

Today many seem to doubt or even deny the existence of absolutes. This lack of conviction has profound consequences because it puts Christianity in conflict with the thinking of the day. Believing in universals or absolutes is essential to believing the gospel. Unfortunately, many people today lack that foundation.

A second presupposition of the Christian faith is the idea that truth is based on thesis and antithesis. This principle is evident in many areas of Christian thinking. However, if you recall, thanks to Hegel, thesis/antithesis has been overrun by the idea that truth is discovered through synthesis. That means the goal of learning is a continual discovery of "new" truth. Obviously, this view of truth and knowing undermines the gospel because the truth we believe is not "new" or yet to be discovered. Rather it has been revealed and we simply need to come to understand and accept it. Another way this continual quest for "new" truth undercuts the gospel is that fixed definitions are hard to agree upon because "truth" is always being created. This thought clearly conflicts with Christian thinking because from a Christian vantage point certain things are fixed and not "evolving."

A third presupposition upon which Christian conviction is based is the reality and existence of both a material and immaterial world. Another way to say it is a seen and unseen world. Many today have a materialist view, in which they see the material as the only real world. Reason and scientific inquiry are the ways to know this world. Faith? It has no place for the materialist. Obviously, this view stands at odds with a Christian worldview because we recognize both spiritual and physical worlds as real and see reason and faith as a means to know.

So far, the point to this chapter is not to give a detailed explanation of how we moved away from a cultural consensus about these key presuppositions (that topic has been addressed in earlier chapters and in far more detail in other works). Rather, it is to raise our awareness that an evangelistic approach that begins from the assumption that there are absolutes or a real material and immaterial world may not be understood. In fact, it may even be ignored or ridiculed in our culture. However, that doesn't mean we cannot communicate effectively, or that somehow we must "change" our message to make it more relevant for today. No, instead, I think we need to be aware of the times in which we live and learn from the example of Paul at Mars Hill in Acts 17.

First, we need to work to understand who we are talking to and how they view the world. Traditional evangelism training often directs us to begin our message talking about God. That's a great place to start if we know the person we're speaking to believes there is a top circle (see Figure 18). However, many people in our day don't believe there is a top circle. They're atheists. If they're agnostic, they're not certain there is a top circle; and, if there is, they're not sure we can know about it. So to first talk to either person about God may seem irrelevant to them. Since very few doubt that man and existence are real, we might be better off to start our conversation from there and eventually move to introduce God into the discussion. Some might think this is avoiding the gospel, but it's not. Rather,

ating a relationship in order to gain the opportunity to share God with them.

How Worldview Is Formed

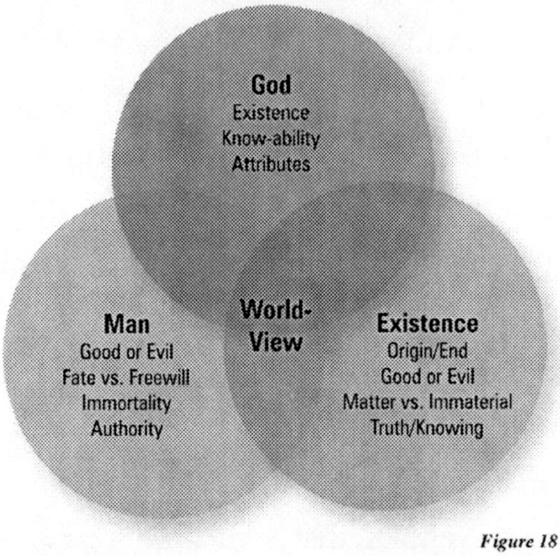

God
Existence
Know-ability
Attributes

Man
Good or Evil
Fate vs. Freewill
Immortality
Authority

World-View

Existence
Origin/End
Good or Evil
Matter vs. Immaterial
Truth/Knowing

Figure 18

Second, we need to be willing to ask questions, before we give answers. In some situations, the Holy Spirit may create the right moment for us to quickly and succinctly share the gospel and we need to seize those opportunities. However, in many circumstances we need to take the time to ask questions to show genuine interest as well as learn their point of view on life. Simply telling people they are wrong doesn't always work at a time where individual opinions are held in such high regard and all viewpoints are considered equally valid or correct. That may seem basic, but we often don't get to the place where we can share the gospel because we don't understand where the disconnect or misunderstanding of Christianity is with the person to whom we are speaking. Furthermore, many non-believers often think Christianity only offers answers to religious questions but is largely irrelevant to the rest of life. This is, of course, not true.

Third, once we understand where a person is coming from, we need to be willing to walk with him to the end of his presuppositions. Then show him how a Christian worldview can provide satisfying answers to life's big questions. Let me give you a word picture and an example that may help clarify the point I am trying to make.

A few years ago my family visited the Grand Canyon and Sedona areas of Arizona. If you've ever been there or seen photographs you know the natural beauty is breathtaking. The combination of unusual rock formations and vivid colors are unlike any other place in the world. One feature of the landscape that really caught my attention was the mesas. Mesas are the land formations that jut out of the landscape and look like stone mushrooms. If you stand on top of one of them, you have a 360° view of the world around you. During our time there, I came to realize that each one of us is like a person standing on a mesa in that we all have a view of the world. The Great Commission compels us to reach that person on the mesa with the gospel. The key question is how do we do that? I would like to suggest that historically, evangelism training has focused on telling the person on the mesa why he or she is wrong and why Christianity

is right. But with the shifts in thinking that have taken place, that approach is often ineffective today. Instead, I believe we need to be willing to move out onto the mesa and walk with the person to the edge of his presuppositions. Then have him look over the edge to see where those presuppositions lead. Having walked along side him, hopefully you gain his trust and then have the opportunity to share your view of the world.

Let me illustrate how this can work by sharing an example from my own life. A few years back, a male neighbor of ours experienced chest pains. He was only in his mid forties, and although it turned out to be non-cardiac related, it was still scary. Following that incident, I had lunch with him and during our conversation I asked if he was afraid of dying when he had his chest pains. He quickly said, "Nah, I've made peace." And I asked, "With who or with what?" He looked at me a bit puzzled, so I asked, "Well, what do you think happens when you die? Without hesitation, he replied, "Worm food! I think you become worm food." "That's interesting," I said. "That *is* one of the ideas man has about what happens when he dies. Can I tell you some of the others?" I asked. "Sure," he said. So I proceeded to tell him that generally man has four main ideas about what happens when you die. Worm food or annihilation is one possibility. Transmigration of the soul or reincarnation is another. A disembodied existence is a third. And finally there is a new embodied existence, which is the Christian worldview. (See the chapter, *Soul and Immortality* for a more detailed discussion.) Then I asked if I could tell him what my view was and why. He said that was fine. So I told him why I didn't think any of the other three answers including "worm food" was satisfying and why I thought an embodied existence was our future. Interestingly, at the end of the conversation, he said, he didn't think "worm food" was his answer any more, but he wasn't sure what the right answer was. So I offered to get together again to discuss the topic further.

Now what I hope you'll see from this example is that my neighbor was like a man standing on a mesa. He had a view of the world that included a thought about life after death. I didn't agree with his view, but I didn't start our discussion there. With conversation, I walked with him looking at death from his conviction till we both could see that it wasn't as satisfying as he thought. Then I offered an opportunity to consider the view of death that Jesus Christ and the Bible provides. Now I wish I could tell you after our dialogue, he fell to his knees there in the restaurant and came to faith in Christ, but he didn't. However, by "walking with him" through conversation, we came to a place where he was open to hear the gospel presented as an answer to a question we all face. Plus, he agreed to meet again and continue the discussion.

Fourth and perhaps most importantly, we must remember that even though we must know how to express a Christian worldview, our goal is never to argue anyone into the kingdom of God. Our goal is to love sacrificially. I Timothy 1:5 says, "The goal of our instruction is love from a pure heart, a good conscience and a sincere faith."[94] That verse is a great reminder that it doesn't matter how much we increase in knowledge if we do not grow in love. In fact, it is sacrificial love and appreciation of others that represent a Christian worldview put in action. One of my favorite examples of this occurred in the life of Augustine, one of the great thinkers and theologians in Western history. Prior to becoming a Christian, Augustine lived a wretched existence but then began to search for answers to life. Initially, his quest led him to a heretical sect called the Manichees, which had a dualistic view of life. Eventually, he came to a relationship with Christ upon hearing the preaching of

Ambrose. However, historian Christopher Hall points out that it wasn't Ambrose's clear articulation of a Christian worldview that first had the greatest impact on Augustine. Hall observes, "Interestingly, it was not Ambrose's ideas that first attracted Augustine, but his character."[95] Augustine, writing in his book *Confessions*, declared, "my heart warmed to him (Ambrose), not at first as a teacher of the truth, which I had quite despaired finding in your Church, but simply as a man who showed me kindness."[96] Here we have Augustine, arguably one of the sharpest minds the Western church has ever produced, first drawn to Ambrose, not by his eloquence or intellect, but his simple kindness.

I pray we never forget that. For though it is good that we learn about the influence of worldview, as we have in this book, we should always remember: it is the way we live, more than what we know, that has the greatest impact on the people around us. For it is then that our worldview is evident to all.

Evangelism is simply one beggar telling another beggar where to find food.

D. T. Niles
Missionary from Ceylon [97]

ENDNOTES

Every reasonable effort has been made to determine copyright holders of excerpted materials. If any copyrighted materials have been inadvertently used without proper credit being given in one form or another, please notify Keith Ogorek (9090 E. State Road 334, Zionsville, IN, 46077) in writing so that future editions may be corrected accordingly.

[1] S. E. Frost, Jr. PhD, *Basic Teachings of the Great Philosophers. A Survey of their Basic Ideas.* (Garden City, NY: Doubleday, 1962, 2nd ed).

[2] *Mars Hill Audio,* Volume 60 Jan./Feb. 2003. http://www.marshillaudio. org/catalog/backtape.asp#vol60.

[3] Ibid.

[4] The Holy Bible: New Revised Standard Version. (Acts 17:16-34). (Nashville, TN: Thomas Nelson, 1989).

[5] James W. Sire, *The Universe Next Door: A Basic Worldview Catalog.* 3rd ed. (Downers Grove, Ill: InterVarsity Press, 1997).

[6] Mortimer J. Adler, *Six Great Ideas. Truth, Goodness, Beauty, Liberty, Equality, Justice. Ideas We Act On.* (New York: Touch Stone, 1997, 4th ed).

[7] S. E. Frost, Jr. PhD, *Basic Teachings of the Great Philosophers. A Survey of their Basic Ideas.* (Garden City, NY: Doubleday, 1962, 2nd ed).

[8] http://www.dictionary.com.

[9] S. E. Frost, Jr. PhD, *Basic Teachings of the Great Philosophers. A Survey of their Basic Ideas.* (Garden City, NY: Doubleday, 1962, 2nd ed).

[10] Ibid.

[11] Alan Hirsch and Eric Rubenstein. "Instant Genius. The Cheat Sheets of Culture," *Philosophy.*(Audio tape) Good Thinking, Inc. 1998.

[12] Ibid.

[13] S. E. Frost, Jr. PhD, *Basic Teachings of the Great Philosophers. A Survey of their Basic Ideas.* (Garden City, NY: Doubleday, 1962, 2nd ed).

[14] Alan Hirsch and Eric Rubenstein. "Instant Genius. The Cheat Sheets of Culture," *Philosophy.* (Audio tape) Good Thinking, Inc. 1998.

[15] Tom Streeter, *Development of Western Thought.* Institute for Christian Thought Seminar: Oct. 9, 2004.

[16] Ibid.

[17] Ibid.

[18] Ibid.

[19] Ibid.

[20] Ibid.

[21] Ibid.

[22] Ibid.

[23] "What Is True," *Forbes ASAP*, October 2, 2000: 225.

[24] Mark A. Noll, *Turning Points. Decisive Moments in the History of Christianity.* (Grand Rapids, Mich: Baker Books, 1997).

[25] Francis A. Schaeffer, *How Should We Then Live? The Rise and Decline of Western Thought and Culture.* (Wheaton, Ill: Crossway Books, 1976).

[26] Mark A. Noll, *Turning Points. Decisive Moments in the History of Christianity.* (Grand Rapids, Mich: Baker Books, 1997).

[27] Francis A. Schaeffer, *How Should We Then Live? The Rise and Decline of Western Thought and Culture.* (Wheaton, Ill: Crossway Books, 1976).

[28] Francis A. Schaeffer, *The God Who Is There.* (Downers Grove, Ill: InterVarsity Press, 1998).

[29] Tom Streeter, *Development of Western Thought.* Institute for Christian Thought Seminar: Oct. 9, 2004.

[30] Francis A. Schaeffer, *How Should We Then Live? The Rise and Decline of Western Thought and Culture.* (Wheaton, Ill: Crossway Books, 1976).

[31] Ibid.

[32] S. E. Frost, Jr. PhD, *Basic Teachings of the Great Philosophers. A Survey of their Basic Ideas.* (Garden City, NY: Doubleday, 1962, 2nd ed).

[33] http://dictionary.reference.com.

[34] S. E. Frost, Jr. PhD, *Basic Teachings of the Great Philosophers. A Survey of their Basic Ideas.* (Garden City, NY: Doubleday, 1962, 2nd ed).

[35] Ibid.

[36] Ibid.

[37] Ibid.

[38] Stanley J. Grenz, *"Answering Pilate. Understanding the Concept of Truth in a Postmodern World,"* Life at Work (Volume 4, Number 2: 61-65).

[39] Allan Bloom, *The Closing of the American Mind.* (New York: Simon and Schuster, 1987).

[40] Bob Francis, *"What Is Postmodernism?"*, Worldwide Challenge (March/April 1999, Volume 26, Number 2, http://www.wwcmagazine.org/1999/postmodern.html).

[41] Mortimer J. Adler, *Six Great Ideas. Truth, Goodness, Beauty, Liberty, Equality, Justice. Ideas We Act On.* (New York: Touch Stone, 1997, 4th ed).

[42] S. E. Frost, Jr. PhD, *Basic Teachings of the Great Philosophers. A Survey of their Basic Ideas.* (Garden City, NY: Doubleday, 1962, 2nd ed).

[43] http://dictionary.reference.com

[44] S. E. Frost, Jr. PhD, *Basic Teachings of the Great Philosophers. A Survey of their Basic Ideas.* (Garden City, NY: Doubleday, 1962, 2nd ed).

[45] Ibid.

[46] Ibid.

[47] A. W. Tozer, *The Pursuit of God. A 31-Day Experience.* (Camp Hill, PA: Christian Publications, 1995)

[48] S. E. Frost, Jr. PhD, *Basic Teachings of the Great Philosophers. A Survey of their Basic Ideas.* (Garden City, NY: Doubleday, 1962, 2nd ed)

[49] Michael D. Lemonick. *How The Universe Will End. Time* (June 25, 2001).

[50] The Holy Bible: New Revised Standard Version. (Rev. 20:7-10). (Nashville, TN: Thomas Nelson, 1989).

[51] The Holy Bible: New Revised Standard Version. (Rev. 21:1-7). (Nashville, TN: Thomas Nelson, 1989).

[52] The Holy Bible: New Revised Standard Version. (Rev. 21:22-25). (Nashville, TN: Thomas Nelson, 1989).

[53] The Holy Bible: New Revised Standard Version. (Heb. 9:27). (Nashville, TN: Thomas Nelson, 1989).

[54] Robert Frost, *New Hampshire: A Poem with Notes and Grace Notes* (New York: Henry Holt, 1923), p. 80. D-11 0397 Fisher Library).

[55] The Holy Bible: New Revised Standard Version. (Psalm 8:3-8). (Nashville, TN: Thomas Nelson, 1989).

[56] Gregory Manchees. *How Apes Became Human.* Time (July 23, 2001: 54–61).

[57] S. E. Frost, Jr. PhD, *Basic Teachings of the Great Philosophers. A Survey of their Basic Ideas.* (Garden City, NY: Doubleday, 1962, 2nd ed).

[58] Ibid.

[59] Ibid.

120

[60] Shakespeare. *Hamlet.*

[61] C. S. Lewis, *Letters to an American Lady.* (Grand Rapids, MI: William B. Eerdmans Publishing Co., 1967).

[62] Shakespeare. *Macbeth.*

[63] S. E. Frost, Jr. PhD, *Basic Teachings of the Great Philosophers. A Survey of their Basic Ideas.* (Garden City, NY: Doubleday, 1962, 2nd ed).

[64] Ibid.

[65] Ibid.

[66] Ibid.

[67] Ibid.

[68] Ibid.

[69] Ibid.

[70] The Holy Bible: New Revised Standard Version. (1 Cor. 15:35-38). (Nashville, TN: Thomas Nelson, 1989).

[71] Jerry Twombly. *The Message of the Stone.* Unpublished poem.

[72] C. S. Lewis. *Mere Christianity.* (Macmillan Pub. Co., November 1952).

[73] S. E. Frost, Jr. PhD, *Basic Teachings of the Great Philosophers. A Survey of their Basic Ideas.* (Garden City, NY: Doubleday, 1962, 2nd ed).

[74] Ibid.

[75] Ibid.

[76] Ibid.

[77] Ibid.

[78] Norman Geisler, *Thomas Aquinas: An Evangelical Appraisal,* (Grand Rapids: Baker, 1991).

[79] The Holy Bible: New Revised Standard Version. (Rom. 12:21). (Nashville, TN: Thomas Nelson, 1989).

[80] A. W. Tozer, *The Pursuit of God. A 31-Day Experience.* (Camp Hill, PA: Christian Publications, 1995).

[81] A. W. Tozer, (Aiden Wilson) Ed, *The Knowledge of the Holy.* (New York: HarperCollins, 1961).

[82] The Holy Bible: New Revised Standard Version. (II Kings 17:24-27). Nashville, TN: Thomas Nelson, 1989).

[83] A. W. Tozer, (Aiden Wilson) Ed, *The Knowledge of the Holy.* (New York: HarperCollins, 1961).

[84] Ibid.

[85] Ibid.

[86] The Holy Bible: New Revised Standard Version. (II Kings 17:24-27). Nashville, TN: Thomas Nelson, 1989).

[87] Ibid.

[88] Ibid.

[89] Ibid.

[90] G. K. Chesterton. *Autobiography*. (Collected Works Vol. 16, p. 212).

[91] Ken Myers. *Mars Hill Audio*, May 2004. http://www.marshillaudio.org/contribute/Spring_04_FR_Letter.pdf.

[92] A. W. Tozer, *The Pursuit of God. A 31-Day Experience*. (Camp Hill, PA: Christian Publications, 1995).

[93] C. S. Lewis, *God In The Dock*. (The Trustees of the Estate of C. S. Lewis, 1970).

[94] The Holy Bible: New Revised Standard Version. (1 Timothy 1:5). Nashville, TN: Thomas Nelson, 1989).

[95] Christopher A. Hall, *Reading Scripture with the Church Fathers*. (Downers Grove, Ill: InterVarsity Press, 1998).

[96] Ibid.

[97] Paul E. Little, *Know Why You Believe*. (Downers Grove, Ill: InterVarsity Press,11th ed, 1976).

Printed in the United States
97365LV00002B/229-300/A

9 781425 953713